Robbing You With A Keyboard Instead Of A Gun

Cyber Crime – How They Do It

Lynn Edgington

Robbing You With A Keyboard Instead Of A Gun

ISBN 9781453895290

Book Cover Design

Book cover and content design by:

eCoverMakers - eBooks, Book Covers, Websites, Marketing.

http://www.eCoverMakers.com

Acknowledgments

"Lynn has been a regular on my show for years, forewarning us about the latest scams and rip-offs, alerting us to the latest online threats and identity theft strategies, and educating us on how to better protect ourselves from crooks and thieves. I'm thrilled that he's finally taken the advice of so many of us and put his insights into book form so that even more people can benefit from his expertise. He's one of the good guys that knows how to not only catch the bad guys, but knows how to prevent them from getting to us. I'm a big fan. You will be too." Frank Pastore, Weekday afternoon drive-time host, 99.5 FM KKLA Los Angeles, author of "Shattered".

This book is an important work at a critical time for both journalists and consumers. It shows how Internet fraud works and how it can be sold by a small group of insiders to an unsuspecting public and it provides a set of standards by which to judge claims of massive rewards for minimum effort. As Abraham Lincoln once said, "It's the old story: You work - I'll eat" which on an individual scale is theft and, in mass, plunder upon the people. David Arnett, Publisher, TulsaToday.com, Radio Host, The David Arnett Show

Rod Cook, MLM WatchDog and MLM Oracle, says this about Lynn Edgington: It is pleasure to talk about Lynn Edgington in this space. Lynn is a dynamite Researcher and one of the main impediments to crooks in the Internet Marketing Space. Lynn's high level of insights into crimi-nal attacks makes him the "go – to man" for any questions about scams or insights into how a rip-off is operated. His dislike of internet criminal activity - combined with his high intelligence makes him and this book a precious commodity. Rod Cook, Bs, MA, MBA

Lynn Edgington's book provides a comprehensive guide on how not to be scammed by criminals like I was. It will force many scam artists into early retirement --- Sam E. Antar (convicted felon, former CPA, and former Crazy Eddie CFO – now a white-collar crime consultant for law en-forcement agencies)

"No one battles the scammers with more resolve than Lynn Edgington. Lynn and Eagle Research Associates are tireless." – PatrickPretty.com

"Having known and worked with Lynn for years now, he is a man who is passionate about truth and justice. I pray with him that this book will rescue many from potential harm." Tom Hollady, Teaching Pastor, Saddleback Church

I have known and worked with Lynn in both a professional and personal capacity for several years. During this time, I have been impressed with his Internet investment fraud knowledge and his ability to communicate and educate the public to its destructive and growing prevalence. Lynn is extremely competent in identifying and assessing Internet investment fraud, Ponzi schemes and related financial scams, and he has an excep-tional ability to connect and communicate their dangers with any audience. However, it is Lynn's commitment and devotion to practicing exemplary business and personal ethics that truly separates him and Eagle Research Associates, Inc. from all others in his field. Jimi Hodge, Sr. Vice President, Kasta, James and Associates

All I can say is wow--what a great job. In His Grip, Barry Minkow, Pastor

To fight fraud, one must be willing to crawl through the convoluted and devious mazes created by scammers and most importantly, outthink the perpetrators. Taking on some of the most complex scams ever invented, Lynn Edgington merely smiles and says, "Make my day." Annie Mc-Guire, Founder and President Emeritus, Fraud Aid, Inc.

"With Mr. Edgington's eagle eyes spotting frauds and scams, and his willing-ness to convey common sense tactics, helps us all keep our earned riches." Rebecca Vizcarra, Associate Director of I.T. Operations and Budgets, Loyola Law School

Dedication

This book is first and foremost dedicated to my incredible wife through whose love, advice, support and encouragement has made Eagle Research Associates, Inc. and this book a reality. She has been there through thick and thin, and kept me focused on the task of writing this book. Thank you Sweetheart for all you mean to me, and for all you have done. You are my inspiration, joy and love of my life.

Second, I would like to thank Tom Holladay, my mentor pastor, who has provided encouragement, prayer support, guidance in the forming of Eagle, and in writing this book. He is always someone you can turn to for guidance, advice, a thoughtful ear, and prayer support. It has meant so much to me to have such a Godly man of integrity and character in my life. You are my hero. Just don't tell Pastor Rick he is my number 2 hero.

Third to Frank Pastore, who has opened so many doors for Eagle, by having me as a regular interview guest on his radio show, The Frank Pastore Show. My very first interview on his show opened the door to having an agent from a federal agency assigned to Eagle Research Associates. From that point forward all our research has been submitted to this assigned agent. There are many doors that have opened for Eagle by my being on his show. To say we are grateful and thankful is an understatement. The success of Eagle is directly tied to my appearance on his show. It is why I owe him so much for all he has done for Eagle. He is a great brother in Christ.

Last but certainly not least is my love and appreciation to members of my Bible study small group: Don & Teri Kennedy, Jerry & Carol Fant, John & Diana Fritch, who are my extended family. Your love, prayers, encouragement, listening, advice, and even prodding (when needed) have helped make this book happen. A special thanks of appreciation to Don & Teri Kennedy who were the first donors to Eagle Research Associates.

Foreword

My elderly father recently placed a significant amount into a scheme that exhibited many of the "red flags" of an investment scam. Smelling a rat, I took immediate and decisive action, and was fortunate to recover his full investment. Like many people, my father worked hard his entire life to squirrel away a small nest-egg, so I was shocked and outraged to discover firsthand that unscrupulous individuals exist who feel no qualms about stealing the fruits of people's labor, even in their latter years. I became an activist and began warning everyone who would listen about the ongoing scam. Despite the warnings from me and others, nearly 4,000 investors were not so fortunate as my father. Most lost their entire investment, which in many cases represented their life's savings. At least one distraught victim took her own life. Three years later, the police finally laid charges against the two individuals at the top of the pyramid, describing the scheme as an egregious $400 million international swindle against ordinary citizens, many of them elderly. No money has yet been recovered for the victims.

Through this ordeal, I witnessed firsthand the merciless and sociopathic tactics of the swindlers and their paid promoters, and observed how, by selling the dream of financial freedom to their victims, the swindlers devoured them in the process. I also observed that, save for a few, the victims refused to accept they had been scammed despite an increasing avalanche of evidence.

People, it seems, are far more vulnerable to being scammed than most of us would like to believe.

Yet knowledge is power, and to be forewarned is to be fore-armed. This book highlights all-too-common scams and frauds, and provides helpful advice on how to sniff out a scam and avoid being "taken". The author, Lynn Edgington, has a heart and a passion for justice, and for exposing, preventing and shutting down these extraordinarily harmful scams. Lynn, like I, has witnessed firsthand the personal devastation for scam victims- and burning with righteous anger, he is fighting back - using the weapons of education, training and awareness. This book is a part of his campaign to defeat the scammers – by training ordinary citizens to identify and walk away from the "Big Lie".

As the saying goes, all it takes for evil to prevail is for good men to do nothing. Lynn is doing something – something big. The world needs more Lynn Edgingtons.

Graham McMillan, San Diego CA

Table of Contents

Can I Really Be Scammed?

Let me ask you a question - Do you believe you can be scammed? If you are like most people, your obvious and immediate answer is "No." Although we like to think not, the truth is we can be scammed, and quite easily in some situations. The problem is that there are so many formats of scams today, people are scammed and they don't even know it until much later.

Most of us like to think of ourselves as being smart enough to recognize a scam when we see it and not fall prey to it. The reality is most of us are wrong. In fact a majority of us have been or will be scammed before this decade is out. In the United States, 1 out of 10 people have been scammed in 2009, or know of someone who was. At the rate these scams are proliferating, it will soon be 1 out of every 8. The Bernard Madoff Ponzi Scheme is proof positive anyone can be scammed. He had professional money managers, nonprofit organizations (whose Board members were astute businessmen/women), and astute investors who were all taken in by Bernard Madoff. Not exactly people considered to be ignorant about investments. So, how does all of this happen? To have a better understanding, we have to go back to the early years of the professional conman/scammer.

In the early years most scams were done in what is known in the trades as a "dog and pony show" or "meet and greet." Simply stated, you were invited to a presentation at a hotel, at a friend's house, or even a churchwhere the host put on a slide show, touted great returns, provided slick brochures, and ensured your investment dollars were safe in the scammers keeping. Some of these programs were touted as tax shelters, others were just offering above average returns in oil and gas ventures, real estate, or prime bank notes that over time would make you a millionaire or a multimillionaire. Because of the limited number of people they could get to come to a presentation, and the time it required to travel from city to city making presentations; they were only able to con people out of a couple of hundreds of millions dollars. I say only, because compared to today's take via the Internet, $200 Million dollars is seen as a minor scam.

Other scams were done through telemarketing campaigns, and especially targeting senior citizens. What the senior citizen, and anyone else, didn't know was when they bit on one of these telemarketing programs, their names were given to other telemarketers; and they ended up getting scammed several times over. To make matters worse, one group portrayed themselves to be an agency that would be able to recover all the money that had been stolen from the previous scam they had fallen prey too. To get their money back would require the victim scammed paying them a fee, of course, as soon as the check cleared never to be heard from again. Thus adding insult to injury.

As the "Baby Boomers" started to mature into the senior citizen ranks, a new tool that was really starting to burst on the scene was the use of the Internet and E-mail. This made it very easy for the scam artist to have a global audience overnight, not just local, and the returns would be even greater for the scam artist. Because you can be anyone on the Internet, tracking these scam artists down is rather difficult. To a technical (techie) computer user they can be found, but for the vast majority of us we have no clue how to find just who these people are or where they are located..

Remember when I said that $200 Million dollars was small potatoes compared to today's take? Well, here are the estimates of the take in 2008 just from Christians and Senior Citizens in Internet Investment scams: $25.8 Billion dollars. Yes, I said "Billion." I said "estimates" because no-one really knows how much because most of the victims of the scam do not report it. Not only have individual Christians been scammed, but also many congregations have lost their church buildings due to these scams; and some of the scams were run by pastors or former pastors. The sad part is the number of Christians and Senior Citizens being targeted and scammed today is still on the rise. Our Jewish brethren are not immune either, as evidenced by the Bernard Madoff Ponzi Scheme that targeted the Jewish Community, and one scam that was run by a Rabbi of all things. Besides Bernie's estimated $65 Billion dollar Ponzi, other scams targeting the Jewish Community have netted close to $3.8 Billion dollars, and we believe the number to be much higher.

Now I know what some of you are thinking. Because I am not a Christian, nor a Senior Citizen, or I am not Jewish, I am safe and have nothing to worry about....right? Well I wish it were true, but it is not. They are also coming after you, and many of you have already been scammed; you just don't know it yet. So who are the other people being targeted by these scammers? Well the majority are people who want to work from home. Whether it is the stay-at-home Mom, or just someone wanting to work from home full-time, or part-time to earn extra income, you are highly susceptible to be scammed. In fact, your E-mail makes you an easy target. Most likely your E-mail is flooded daily with work from home offers, you've won the lottery, a dying widow needs your help, a payment processor is needed, etc. you know the kinds I am talking about. And now a new breed of scam E-mails are fooling people, like you, into becoming a victim. They are the bank phishing E-mail scams.

You receive an E-mail saying your bank account has been compromised, or there has been suspicious activity in your account, and they want you to confirm your account information is correct. They are so kind to even include a link to your bank account for your convenience. The only problem is that the link is not your bank account, but a fake account that looks **exactly** like your bank's website. They then steal your banking information (your username, and pin number/access code). By the time you realize it is not your bank's URL, they have already cleaned out your bank accounts. Congratulations, you have now become a victim of a scam. Those scams that were targeting Affinity Groups (people from an identifiable group) are the same scams that also target you.

With interest rates at an almost all-time low most Money Market, Bonds and Certificates of Deposit are not as attractive as they once were. So many people are looking for alternative investments to increase their rate of return. Congratulations, you just joined the biggest group scammers have targeted in parting you from your money.

So this problem is primarily an U.S. problem right? While it is true significant amounts of money has been scammed from U.S. Citizens, it is global in reach just as the Internet is global in reach. *Research published in the U.K. by the Office of Fair Trading* shows nearly half of the U.K. adult population had been targeted by a scam in 2007. One in 15 people (3.2 million adults) in the U.K. fall victim to a scam involving deceptive unsolicited mailings, phone calls, or E-mails. The government reveals the true cost of scams in the

UK at £3.5 Billion per year (and rising), or roughly £850 per citizen on average. Scammers don't just limit their audience to the U.S. and the UK. Almost every country in the world today has had its citizens taken in by scammers, especially in the last three years. According to estimates from various groups, the global amount scammed was $500 Billion Dollars in 2009, with the U.S. having the lion's share of $300 Billion Dollars; startling figures to say the least. Remember, this is thought to be at least 40% under-reported. So what is a scam, how can I recognize it when I see it, what can I do about it?

First we need to explain some terminology we will be using in describing various scams. Each of these will be explained in greater detail later.

Ponzi/Ponzi Scheme Scams: The most common term used in an investment scam is called a Ponzi, or Ponzi scheme. The name Ponzi comes from Charles Ponzi, a swindler from the early 1900s who conned $10 Million from investors by promising them a 40% return on their investment. Any program that resembles this scam thus earns the name Ponzi or Ponzi scheme.

A Ponzi scheme is essentially an investment fraud wherein the operator promises high financial returns or dividends not available through traditional investments. Instead of investing victims' funds, the operator pays "dividends" to initial investors using the principle amounts "invested" by subsequent investors.

The scheme generally falls apart when the operator flees with all of the proceeds, or when a sufficient number of new investors cannot be found to allow the continued payment of "dividends" to the initial early investors.

Internet Investment Scams: These take many different forms, and with many different financial products. They can be offering Reverse Pension Plans, Prime Bank Notes, FOREX Trading, Auction Trading, Fake Designer Goods, Private Placement Offerings, Sports Arbitrage Betting, or in some cases they never reveal what type of investments they are offering; just that they are getting phenomenal returns. In short they are asking you to just *"Trust Them."*

Private Bank Notes Scams: Here you are led to believe that only the wealthy take advantage of these huge money makers that are notes from the worlds top 100 banks that can be bought at discount and then sold for a huge profit when they mature. This is a myth. They don't exist contrary to what the scammer will tell you.

Work From Home Scams: These usually fall into what is known as the advance fee scam. A company in Europe, China, Malaysia, etc., is expanding into the US and they need a transfer agent to handle his or her account receivables. You are to collect money from their customer's, deposit the money into your bank account, retain 10% or 20% for your trouble, and then wire them the difference.

Or they take the form of being an intermediary in receiving goods, inspecting them for damage, and then forwarding them on to a third party. For this you will be paid a small percentage of the total costs of the goods being forwarded.

There are: the medical/legal transcription service, customer service survey takers, mystery shopper, or setting appointments. Others offer you the opportunity to become an E-bay reseller, or the Google Work From Home scams. There are so many of these it would be almost impossible to list, and if I did the list would be outdated before this was printed. That is how rapidly these Google work from home scams are proliferating.

Cash Gifting Schemes: These go by different names (2 Up, Charitable giving, Cycling Programs), but generally they follow these guidelines: You gift money to someone who is above you on a list or pyramid, and in turn you have others sign up under you, and your name ends up in the top slot and when it does thousands will be sent to you by all those below you. Want more money, just do it over and over again. They are all illegal.

Nigerian 419 E-mail Scams: If you have an E-mail account, you have probably received hundreds of these types of E-mails. These types of E-mail scams take many different forms, but all have the same story line, just different circumstances: Someone has died, you are to stand in as the beneficiary; or a Christian is dying, cannot trust family, you are to help them distribute their wealth among charitable organizations as they don't have enough time to live to do it themselves; or your company, or you as a contractor/consultant, was found to have outstanding invoices that can now be paid. This scam is often referred to as the 4-1-9 scam, ironically after section 4-1-9 of the Nigerian Penal Code that relates to fraudulent schemes.

You Have Won the Lottery E-mail Scams (also part of the Nigerian 419 Scam):   You are told your E-mail has won you millions of dollars in a lottery. To collect your winnings you have to contact their fiduciary agent, provide them with your personal information, and pay processing fees for you to claim your winnings.

Bank/Credit Card Phishing Scams: Here you receive an E-mail from a bank, financial institution, or credit card company claiming you need to update your personal information as someone has tried to access your account, or they have noticed unusual activity on your account. They provide you a link to click for you to update your information.

Phony Job Scam: You are notified that your resume you have posted on one of the major job sites is of interest to them. They have a position they believe you are qualified for as their courier or agent and offer you a job on the spot. You will be receiving large checks, depositing them in your account, take out your fee, and send the balance on to the company. Or they saw your resume on Monster or Craigslist and before you come in for an interview they want you to have your credit report done.

Affinity Fraud: Affinity Fraud refers to investment scams that prey upon members of identifiable groups such as: religious or ethnic communities, senior citizens, or even professional groups. They target the leaders of these various types of groups to join to spread the word of the investment fraud giving it legitimacy and validity to members of the group targeted.

Pay-to-Click or Ad Surfing Scams: The premise is to join an advertising company as a member to advertise your business on their website. You pay a set amount to advertise your website, and pay a monthly fee to share in the revenue of the company. To share in the revenue you must also surf other ads on their website in 15 second intervals for a few minutes or hours per day. You will receive a daily percentage of your advertising purchase cost back in rebates. You can also earn referral fees for having others join under you in the program.

E-mail Chain Letters Scams: Instead of using the US Post Office delivery system as in the olden days, this is now making the rounds on the Internet. This is the letter form of online Cash Gifting.

Penny Stock Pump and Dump Scams: You receive an E-mail touting a stock that will explode in price, yet it can be bought for just a few cents on the dollar right now. The company will make an announcement that will cause the stock to explode raising the stock price 200-2,000% when released, and now is the time for you to buy.

HYIP Programs: These are programs that provide high yields, but claim little or no risk is involved. They usually claim to be investing in Oil and Gas, FOREX, Sports Arbitrage Betting, Buying Stock in under-valued companies, and one even claimed it was from loan-sharking....or as they said, "Financial Mercenaries."

NON-HYIP Programs: These offer above average rate of returns, but are associated with lower risk type of investments such as Pension Plans, Endowment Plans, Real Estate, Alternative Energy, Prime Bank Notes, Private Placements, and advertising programs.

Fake MLM/Network Marketing/Pyramid Programs: We have all heard of Amway/Quixtar, and many of us have now heard of Monavie, Pre-Paid Legal, Acai Plus, Arbonne International, HerbalLife, to name a few legitimate MLM programs. The fake MLM/Network Marketing programs claim to have a product, but in reality there is no product. All you are doing is signing up people, and all you are receiving is the referral fees for the people who join under you. This is called a classic Pyramid Scam.

Now there are many more scams than these, but these represent the majority of the scams you will be exposed to on an almost daily basis. I started out asking you: "Can I really be scammed?" As the statistics show, YES you can. In the ensuing chapters, we will identify each type of scam, what they look like, explain how they do it, who are all the players involved to make it happen, how they lure you in, and what red flag warning signs to look out for. Additionally, you will see how to do basic due diligence, and how to protect yourself.. In essence you will see what really is happening versus what you think is happening, so you can educate yourself from becoming a victim of a scam.

Next, the anatomy of a scam.

The Anatomy of a Scam – What Does A Scam Look Like?

In this and subsequent chapters, we will examine the anatomy of a scam, and how each of these scams work. You will have a chance to see just what each of these types of scams look like as well as get a feel for why so many people bought into the scam in the first place. What happens when the scam starts collapsing and how they continued to defend the program to the bitter end. These scams fall into two categories: Non-HYIP and HYIP. But first, let's define the players who composed the scam.

THE PERPETRATOR/ADMIN OF THE SCAM: The person who created the scam, and in many cases also takes the role of the administrator, herein called admin, for the program. This is your contact person for all issues to be resolved, provides updates, handles the transfer of money, maintains the website, and usually the program will have its own internal forum for members which the admin moderates.

THE PROMOTERS: No scam would be successful without the "Promoters" of these scams. They are the ones who go to all the financial forums, begin a forum discussion about the program, and of course swear to the legitimacy of the program. They are what are called the "shills"' "pimps," and "referral hounds" of the scam. Their job is to recruit as many people as possible into the scam, get as many in their down-line, and to run interference when someone starts questioning the scam's legitimacy. The people who dare question the scam are called "naysayers," "trolls," or "negative thinkers" to name a few of the names they are called by the promoter's and administrators of these programs. They are also called "jealous, afraid to take risks, dark Christians, and other unflattering comparisons to dictators, butchers, and despots.

The promoters do their best to not allow the naysayer, trolls, negative thinkers to gain a foothold in the public financial forums. They always vouch for the "admin" saying how honest they are, how trustworthy they are, and how they have only the best interest of the members at heart. They also lead the charge of claiming they are being paid, being paid on-time, and will continue to do so for a long time to come. Some even invoke "God" into their conversation on the forums at some point to demonstrate they are a Christian, and would not be part of any illegal program or scam. Usually when this happens, it means the scam is about to implode or be shut-down by the government. In short, it is in trouble, but they are trying to mask the trouble. Some of these "promoter's" are individuals, and many times they represent a group of investors in which they are the head of the group.

What most don't know about the Promoter is that they are the first ones in and the first ones out of the program long before it folds and disappears.
They make most of their money off the number of referrals they get to sign up under them in the program. Their initial investment is usually guaranteed by the admin/person running the scam. Once it is returned, they no longer have any money "invested" in the program, and continue to be paid their referral bonus. But to the outsider it appears they are still invested just like them in the program. So when the program crashes, they have not lost any money unlike the people they referred and convinced the program was legitimate and would last a long time to come. More on this later.

THE FINANCIAL FORUMS: where these programs advertise, are listed and promoted. The Forum Owner accepts advertising money for the program to be prominently displayed when entering the forum, as well as on each thread (individual links for each program being offered) where people post about the program, and of course, where the Promoter's encourage others to join the program.

THE FINANCIAL ONLINE NEWSLETTERS: The owners of these newsletters interview the admin of the program providing them a platform to announce their program and encourage people to sign-up in the program. They are paid to interview the admin and give a glowing report about the program.

PAYMENT PROCESSORS: None of these scams could operate without the payment processors. These are organizations that provide the exchange between currencies. They charge both parties, the scam program and the investors, a fee for their services to exchange currencies, both incoming and outgoing payments. They are called offshore as they are domiciled outside the United States. The most popular payment processors used by the scam programs operate out of Canada; but are located all over the world. More on their role later when I explain how they do it. Here is an example of how a Non-HYIP and HYIP format are blended together in a typical Ponzi scheme/scam.

THE INVESTMENT PONZI

One would think that after almost 90 years, people would not fall for this type of scam. A Ponzi just means that early investors in a program are paid from new investors' funds joining the program; not from returns on the investment. Many of the Internet Investment Ponzi's combine the Non-HYIP and the HYIP programs into one that allows them to achieve their 'claimed' results. Whatever underlying investment is being touted as the security providing the return either does not exist or represents only a small portion of the funds invested. When the number of new members cannot continue paying for all those who joined before them, the system collapses. It also can be called a pyramid. Most Ponzi schemes center on financial instruments. The most common types are: real estate, investment offers, prime bank notes, reverse pension plans, commodity trading, FOREX, oil and gas, IPO (Initial Public Offering) and even charitable fund raising.

A typical combination of Non-HYIP and HYIP Ponzi program: This consists of several different types of investments that will appeal to the masses. First you have an investment program that will provide higher than normal returns from most securities. The pitch is that they have found a way to level the playing field, and it is now time for the "little guy" to finally have a shot at the brass ring. They will be able to take advantage of what previously only the wealthy could avail themselves to in the financial world. They would finally be able to get out of debt and live the good life just like the rich. The best part is it will be done with a minimal amount to invest thus making it easy for all to participate. And to make the sales pitch even more appealing, and not just centered on greed, they say will take a percentage of all returns and do charitable works around the world to the needy and starving people living in poverty. They also prey on those conspiracy theorists. These are the people who believe the government does not want their citizens to be wealthy, so they can continue to keep them in poverty, bondage or serfdom as this group claims.

Here in a nutshell you have the reason the Christian Community, the Jewish Community, Senior Citizens, and Americans are targeted. The Judeo-Christian community as a whole are the most giving, trusting, compassionate, and caring people. They will give to others before spending on themselves. They trust people who want to help others, and they especially want to help the less fortunate among us. They also represent about 85% of the American population. Senior Citizens (comprised mostly of Christians and Jews) are looking for ways to supplement their retirement income, and at the same time giving back to their community or charities. Americans are the most giving people on the face of the earth. America is the first in and the last out with supplies, money and people to help at every world disaster. The program I outlined above meets each of these human traits. Now you know why it is so easy to be taken in by the scammers if you are Christian, Jewish, Senior Citizen, or just an average American.

What you also have to understand is that the people who run these scams are almost in every case a sociopath. Sociopaths have no heart, no conscience and no remorse. They think nothing of lying, cheating and stealing. Socio-paths often blend easily into society. They're entertaining and fun at parties. They appear to be intelligent, charming, well-adjusted and likable. The key word is "appear." Because for sociopaths it's all an illusion, designed to convince you to give them what they want. Sociopaths are masters of manipulation. Sociopaths are prolific scammers. Scammers will honor their commitments in the beginning so that you begin to trust them. They will appear to be unselfishly helping other people. Their objective is to get you to drop your guard. They use the same sales pitches used by salesmen designed to convey confidence in their program, safety, security, and trust. When in reality none of it is true. The Internet is custom-tailored for sociopaths. It provides them with unlimited opportunities to manipulate and defraud people.

Here is how a typical Ponzi investment scam is presented to lure you into participating:

Format #1: "The founder's reason for offering the program preys on becom-ing wealthy and the conspiracy theory:

The stated purpose of our Program, and my personal philosophy and commitment, is to empower average citizens, the little guy, and help them free themselves from the financial servitude in today's society; and economic structures that have been cast upon them."

Format #2: "The conspiracy theory as the purpose of offering the program:

It is time for the average guy to be finally able to grab the brass ring. The rich, the banking community, and the government have for too long been able to keep the average guy down. The purpose of this program is to level finally the playing field, and for the average guy to invest in programs that only the rich could access for so long. Not only will you be able to achieve financial independence, but you will also be contributing to help the poor through our charitable giving program to improve their living conditions, environment, and health around the globe."

The pitch by both goes something like this for an investment program:

"Our investment strategy is to maximize the investment return, while minimizing risk. To achieve this, we use a tried and tested strategy of investing in leading and diverse markets worldwide such as private equity funds, Bonds, Forex, Derivatives, IPO's, Finance and Property and co-investing in direct investments with selected fund managers. We have a proactive management style to identify leading fund managers and opportunities for investment in fund and direct investments. Portfolio's are diversified by country, stage, size of investment and industry sector.

We profit from our knowledge in private equity funds worldwide and our main investment focus is on expansion capital. This sector of the market has consistently produced the best investment returns and according to expert opinion, will continue to provide an excellent volume of high quality deal opportunities. We will also make highly selective commitments to technology opportunities and secondary funds where these have the clear potential for investment out-performance. Because of our expertise, you will be able to achieve exceptional returns on your investment. "We can achieve 2% per trading day compounded on your investment guaranteed," and we don't even have 100% of your investment dollars at work to obtain and sustain these results."

After reading these statements, I am sure your first impression was: "Wow!" This is exciting and finally I will be able to get ahead financially. Where do I sign up and how much money can I invest to obtain these returns? Many of you do not even suspect that what you have just read, while sounding incredibly good, cannot be achieved. And of course there are testimonials of people who claim they are in the program and have received payments demonstrating the program is legitimate. Then you have the urging of your friend or family member who joined encouraging you to join too. This is your dream come true, your ability to receive untold riches, all legitimate, and for little or no work on your part. Just refer people into the program and you can make even more money.

Now let's analyze the statements made for this program, and see just how it all starts unraveling when you start asking questions, or by doing your due diligence before you get all caught up in the hype and join. Remember the stated **"<u>guaranteed</u> rate of return is 2% per trading day compounded.**

Let's take the first sentence:

"Our investment strategy is to maximize the investment return, while minimizing risk."

I would certainly hope so as this is what everyone is looking for in an investment. You want significant returns, but you also want your risk low so you don't lose a significant portion of your principal. When you first read that statement about their investment strategy, you probably interpreted **"maximize the investment return"** as **"high return."** Most of us do. Only problem is: The higher the return the greater the risk. If they didn't say this, you would not be as interested in investing your hard earned money.

Now the next sentence is the crux of the program:

"To achieve this, we use a tried and tested strategy of investing in leading and diverse markets worldwide such as private equity funds,

Bonds, Forex, Derivatives, IPO's, Finance and Property and co-investing in direct investments with selected fund managers."

This sounds impressive, and it is meant to be. Most people have no clue what all these types of investments are, how they work, and if they can provide the return claimed by the program. While you may have heard of some of these programs, most really don't understand how they work, or what risks they incur to participate. Yet you have the Promoters telling you how great the program is, they have been paid like clockwork, and this is your chance to achieve financial independence or riches beyond your dreams and desires.

If you have a tried and tested program, it means just that. It has been tested and refined to obtain a set objective, and it has been tried and proven to work. Not once, not twice, but consistently; and it has to have been tried over a period of at least a year to demonstrate it works the majority of the time it is tried. No investment program will be right 100% of the time. They don't exist. But if it is a true "tried and tested" program, you will make more than you lose more than 60% of the time.

So just what are these types of investments the program claims they are investing into providing you the guaranteed rate of return they promised? But more important can they?

All of the types of investing named would very difficult to explain in complete detail for you to understand them. It is because several are very technical and have numerous facets to them, thus making it very difficult to explain them completely. To do so would make this book exceed War and Peace in length, and it would probably confuse you even more due to information overload. I will provide a synopsis of a few of the investment vehicles of the program so you can get a flavor of the risks involved as well as why many of these programs could not even come remotely close to providing that **2% per day compounded being guaranteed.**

Private Equity Funds: Sounds really impressive and somewhat a little mysterious at the same time, doesn't it? Only problem is that they are very difficult to purchase as they are private and not publicly traded. You have to know someone who wants out of his or her position, and then be financially able and willing to buy it at the price he or she wants. You must also meet the "Qualified Investor" rule, and they are also a long-term investment. Simply put, you must hold usually for more than three years and in many cases ten years or more. To be a Qualified Investor means you must have a specified annual salary, assets, excluding houses and cars, of a certain amount, you have net income to cover your day-to-day living expenses, and by investing would not cause you any financial hardship if you lost your funds. The average return for this type of investment over its life span is around 30%, which is considered exceptionally good. Not going to provide you *the guaranteed high daily 2% rate of return compounded on your investment* this fraudulent program is promoting.

Bonds: This is a subject that many more of you are familiar with and have some understanding of how they work. Only problem with this type of investment is that again it is a long term investment. Bill Gross, the head of PIMCO, is recognized as one of the worlds top bond traders, and in most circles the top bond trader in the world. He has achieved some of the highest returns (10%-12%) on bond portfolios of any trader in the markets today. Still, even as good as he is, in this market, his returns wouldn't even come close to the *high 2% daily guaranteed return compounded* being promoted by this fraudulent program.

Forex trading: Of all the investments listed, this is one of the most exotic, high risk, but can return the highest daily rate of return, other than Derivatives, of all the investment programs listed. To be successful in this market requires a trader that trades 24/7. Real Forex trading usually deals with: currencies, gold, silver, and precious metals; with the most prevalent being currencies. In these trades you are looking for a variance in the rate of exchange from one market to the next. In short, you try to find it trading at a lower price (rate of exchange) on one market and trading at a higher price (rate of exchange) on another market; by buying low and selling high. The only problem with this market is these offsets in market price only last for a very brief moment, usually within minutes and sometimes in matters of seconds. Even with a successful trader, you cannot sustain a *high 2% daily guaranteed return compounded* on your investments in this market. Just so you know, *2% per trading day compounded guaranteed* would be an **annual rate of return of 14,400%** on your investment. To my knowledge the best any FOREX trading has achieved is an annual rate of 660%. A far cry from

14,400% (annualized basis) a 2% daily rate of return program would generate, but still an incredible rate of return.

Are you starting to get the picture of how it sounds good to the ear, but falls flat when truly investigated? I sure hope so. Now for the really fun topic, Derivatives:

Derivatives: The name itself conjures up images of high dollar stakes, the ability to make a lot of money in a very short period, and all the other buzz words that make the heart flutter with excitement and anticipation. The only problem is these products are so volatile and unpredictable, that they can ruin you financially.

So what is a Derivative anyway? A derivative is a generic term for specific types of investments from which payoffs over time are "derived" from the performance of assets (such as commodities, shares or bonds), interest rates, exchange rates, or indices (such as stock market index, consumer price index [CPI], or an index of weather conditions). This performance can determine both the amount and the timing of the payoffs. The diverse range of potential underlying assets and payoff alternatives leads to a huge range of derivatives contracts available to be traded in the market. The main types of derivatives are futures, forwards, options, and swaps. I am sure that you all fully understand what a Derivative is now. While I am being somewhat facetious here, at least you have the general terms of just what they are.

So just how dangerous are they? Do any of you remember Barings Bank and Nick Leeson? Nick, who was a trader at Barings Bank, incurred a $1.3 Billion Dollar loss that bankrupted the centuries old bank. So how did he manage to do this? By trading in the derivates markets is how. Getting the idea they might be a little risky? No? How about the largest municipal bankruptcy in recorded History in Orange County, California of $1.6 Billion Dollars from trading in derivatives? But let's not also forget the bankruptcy of Long-Term Capital Management, also trading in derivatives, which followed just three months after the OC Bankruptcy. Hopefully by now you get the picture that while you can make significant returns on your investments in derivatives, you can also lose your shirt, literally. Still even with all the high returns this market can provide, you cannot guarantee 2% per trading day return on your investment, let alone compounded.

IPO's: This stands for Initial Public Offering. While you can make a lot of money off an initial public offering initially, over the long run it is usually not sustainable for any long period. It certainly is not close to generating a 2% per trading day return on your investment, as promoted in this program. While there are some exceptions to this rule, they are far and few in between, and you have to guess right every time. Even with that all happening, they come nowhere close to providing such a high daily trading day rate of return.

By now you should understand the other investment programs listed cannot provide this rate of return, either. No need to go into detail on what they are, and how they work. As for the rest of the statements, they are designed to impress, convince you they know what they are doing, and to instill confidence of your money being in good hands.

While on the surface the opportunity presented sounded plausible and sustain the returns promised, upon closer examination we discovered there was no way any of these investments alone, or in conjunction with each other could *provide the guaranteed return of 2% per day compounded.* The essence of a really good scam is 3% truth, and 97% lie; but the lie sounds better than the 3% truth. If a trader really could generate a guaranteed 2% per day compounded, every high net-worth individual and corporation would have him trading for them; and them alone. Yes it is possible to make a 400% return in one day playing high yield investments like commodities, FOREX, arbitrage, and options, but it cannot be sustained day-in and day-out for any length of time. To obtain 2% compounded per day means you would have to be right 100% of the time in these markets, and simply impossible to do. For every time you could make 2,000% in one day trading, you could also lose that and much more the very next day; and it has happened. It is why it is called HIGH RISK. The best known annual return in the High Yield Investments markets was 660%. By the way, the same traders who managed this feat could not duplicate it the next year. In fact their return for the next year was only 38%. An excellent annual rate of return, to say the least, but a far cry from the 660% rate of return from the previous year. It is not a sure thing, and not sustainable daily, weekly, monthly let alone year in and year out.

The name of this program was PIPS (People In Profit Systems), and run by Bryan Marsden, a British citizen and his Malaysian wife, Sharon. Bryan Marsden claimed he had discovered a formula he had to keep secret, which obtained this guaranteed 2% per day compounded rate of return. All of this from a person who had never had any investment experience in his life as a broker or trader. His bio said he was a successful electrician contractor and consultant. All of the companies he claimed he had completed contracts for had no record of his ever doing any kind of work for them. So even his work experiences were suspicious, and believed to be fabricated. PIPS was raided by Bank Negara Malaysia in the fall of 2005 confiscating all their computers and shutting the company down. In October 2006 the Marsden's were arrested and charged with more than 105 combined charges of bank fraud, wire fraud and operating two illegal Internet companies. They did not make bail, and remained in jail through their two trials. Their trials started in late 2008, and continued due to delays into the fall of 2009 when they abruptly pleaded guilty. They were sentenced to 5 years in prison, and given credit for their time already served awaiting trial. They were released in early 2010. Now before you think you would never fall for this, more than 80,000 people worldwide did. The odds are that some of you reading this book were one of them. I will explain other types of the Non-HYIP and HYIP later in this book.

Next, preying on desperation.

Preying On Desperation

What is sad is in today's economy, scammers are taking advantage of people's desperation, fear, and concern for their future. We have seen a 401(k) becoming a 201(k)'s or worse, retirement savings barely covering living expenses, medical costs rising, as well as the values of homes declining to below their loan value. Sad to say but this is the exact scenario the scammer thrives on. It makes their job much easier to con you into buying into their scam. And this is happening globally, not just here in the U.S. With the Internet, scams are global in scope and prey on the public worldwide.

One of the largest new types of scam to hit the Internet has been the Reverse Pension Plan or RPP for short. What has made them so attractive is their low dollar cost to enter and the promise of high return. There have been at least 20 of these introduced, but the largest of these is Global Pension Plan with more than 350,000 members. They know people are desperate, and so they will easily fall for the sales pitch.

Here are some examples (with typos, misspelled words and grammatical errors as material was taken from their official website or from the introduction posts on the financial forums) of other type of programs that preyed upon people's desperation:

GNI:

GNI is based around gambling on sporting events. Not just gambling but arbitrage betting. In simplified terms that's taking advantage of the fact that different bookmakers will always offer you different odds on any given sporting event. Arbitrage betting involves spreading the bet between different bookmakers to then ensure that you will have one winning bet regardless of the outcome and that this winning bet will not only cancel the losses from the other bets, but leave you with a handsome profit for your efforts

An arbitrage opportunity in sports betting or other events means that one is able to bet on all possible outcomes of a certain match or event at odds that guarantee profit regardless of who wins that match or event. This is not gambling – it's just a market phenomenon based on pure mathematics and occurs when bookmakers have different opinions on the result of a certain game or event. There is absolutely no risk involved for our members! Principal is guaranteed.

We are currently offering two investment plans. Our daily plan is offering a variable profit of 0.7-1.1% daily, on average over the past couple of months it was around 1% daily and a weekly plan with a profit of 6%. The minimum to deposit is $20 for the daily plan and $100 for the weekly plan.

The main difference is that our members can understand what we are doing with their hard earned money. Our project is for each and every of our members translucent and comprehensible. We are paying a decent and steady return for a long time now and don't have months of principal lock-up.

Pathway-To-Prosperity/P-2-P

"P-2-P Network" is a long term "private" investment program, investing in various online and offline activities. Profits from these investments are shared with Members and invested in stable long term investments, to guarantee our program's stability for the long term. The Minimum allowed for investing and withdrawals is $10.00 USD. It's time to finally stop worrying about not making money on the internet. "P-2-P Network" has developed a system that put your investments on Autopilot with the ONLY TRULY Automated System that's affordable for everyone! "P-2-P Network" is an investment strategy based on allowing ordinary investor's access to higher returns by using all the resources available to global investors.
.

We diminish the risks normally associated with these types of investments by pooling your money and spreading the investments across a diverse range of global opportunities such as bonds, IPOs, finance & property, private equity funds, forex, co-investing in direct investments and private placement investment funds etc. We will assist you by allowing your funds to "piggy-back" on ours... returns earned in the "P-2-P Network" Private Fund is totally out of reach for the average individual!!

Now you can achieve financial independence without relying on others joining the program after you, although once you start to enjoy the rewards of "P-2-P Network" you will want to tell all your friends and we do offer handsome referral commissions for the term that they invest in the plan. After all, all we really want to do is use our "hard-earned-cash" to create a better living for ourselves, our families, our loved ones ..... and now, since we have gone public with "P-2-P Network" ...... for ALL of our valued Members !!

IMPORTANT NOTE: This is NOT a H.Y.I.P. site... We do NOT believe in them! You must stay away at all costs!

Name Value Runtime Return R.I.* Interest every

7 Day Plan 10.5 %

15 Day Plan 26.25 %

30 Day Plan 60 %

60 Day Plan 150 %

Thirty Dollar Unit/TDU

THIRTY $ UNITS HAS IT ALL, WILL PROVIDE IT ALL, AND IS INVITING YOU TO JOIN IN NOW. DON'T BE LEFT OUT!!

Do you want to earn $12,500 for every $30.00 unit you buy?

This is an outstanding deal!! You simply cannot go wrong by joining this program. This is NOT- MLM Network Marketing- NOT a busi-

ness, NOT Selling or buying products and not gifting. This is NOT one of those reverse pension plans. It is: An Humanitarian group who in turn, over a short period of time, pays a high rate of interest.

A unit is $30.00. You can purchase as many units as you like. You don't have to refer anyone to participate in this program, but for every person that you refer you will receive $50.00 per person per unit. EXAMPLE: If your person purchases 5 units that's $250.00 more for you!!

We have decided to up the payout for all members that have 2 or more referrals! Now, instead of the normal $12,500, you will receive $17,500 for every unit that you have purchased! Keep up the good work!

Referrals Payout per Unit

0-1: $12,500 2-3: $17,500 4-5: $22,500 6 +: $ 27,500

Genius Funds:

Our funds are investing mainly in highly lucrative equities and bonds, focusing on emerging economies. We offer investment products that provide flexibility, keeping pace with the individual demands of our investors. You can invest with as little as $10 into the Emerging Markets Growth Fund and the World Bond Market Fund.

Fund name Symbol Dividends

Emerging Markets Growth Fund EMGF 1.0% - 1.9%, Daily payments

World Bond Market Fund WBMF 5.5% - 8.5%, Weekly payments

'Genius CD'. It is meant for investors who are looking for a medium-income, short-term investment. The term of the investment is three months and the interest is fixed at 6% per month, 18% per term while the investment term on shares of the funds lasts from 150 to 180 days from purchase and income ranges from 5 to 9 percent per week.

GENIUS HIGH-INTEREST DEPOSIT ACCOUNT

Have you been looking for a high-yield deposit account with flexible terms of investment? The Genius High Yield Deposit Account, or HYDA, combines one of the highest returns in the industry with the flexibility of your local bank account. Minimum deposit is $300. If your balance falls below $300, your HYDA account stops earning interest.

Genius HYDA is a fixed interest deposit account. There is no term of deposit on the account, which means that you can withdraw funds from your account at any time. The interest is payable daily. A ten-day notice must be given prior to withdrawal from Genius HYDA.

Interest rates:

$300-$2,000	14%	Monthly
$2,001-$5,000	18%	Monthly
$5,001-$50,000	25%	Monthly

We offer a competitive referral program that pays 6% for referral of a customer that purchases shares in an investment fund and 3% for referral of a customer that invests into our Genius CD account.

DRFund:

This program has been created to help many people earn from revenue streams that usually require high capital to participate. We wanted to brings these to you, real offline revenue sources as a safe and reliable way to earn from your deposits.

Paying 20% each month

LEVEL ONE: *$20/month - Basic Business Member*

Basic members may deposit up $2500 USD to earn 20% per month for a total of 240%

LEVEL TWO: $40/month ? Premier Business Member

Premier members may deposit up to $5000 USD to earn 20% per month for a total of 480%

LEVEL THREE: $60/month ? Benefactor Business Member ?

Benefactor members may deposit up to $10,000 USD to earn 20% per month for a total of 720%

LEVEL FOUR: $120/month? Foundations Business Member Pays to level 8 8% 8 levels down.

Foundations members may deposit up to $25,000 USD to earn a minimum of 20% per month for A total of 1200%

The minimum deposit for The DR Fund NOT including the matrix is $50 USD. To earn a 20% return per month from your investment, there is a required 3x8 matrix membership to join.

MATRIX

LEVEL ONE: Pays to level 5. 8% 5 levels down

LEVEL TWO: Pays to level 6. 8% 6 levels down

LEVEL THREE: Pays to level 7. 8% 7 levels down

LEVEL FOUR: $120 Pays to level 8 8% 8 levels down

Human Capital Insurance-25 /HCI

The fee has been set to $42. There will be an extra 7% added which we will charge for the work that has been put into this and for the contacts that we are offering regarding this opportunity, so the total *amount to be paid is $45. According to the contract of the fund each beneficiary will have the possibility to hold 15 positions in the fund, which then will total at $675, no more then 15 is allowed. (emphasis mine) Each beneficiary will at the end (this will take place 6-8 weeks after we have reached 27,000 beneficiaries) receive a one time payment of £42 500 (About $78 000). Please also note that the fee will be paid back to the beneficiary if the project isn't fulfilled for any reason. We will however keep our administrative fee of 7%.*

Later in their summary of the plan they say this: Administrative fee for the current Pension/Lifeinsuranceplan as explained: $45 (For 3 positions, $ 135, for 6 position $ 270, for 9 positions $ 405, for 15 positions $ 675, and 20 positions $900).   So much for no more than 15 are allowed.

We have set up a bonus system in one level, which is what is allowed according to the banks / institutes, which will pay every beneficiary an amount of £1900 (About $3500) for every new beneficiary that is put into the project.

The process of transferring the funds will start once we have reached 27 000 beneficiaries. The amount mentioned above that is being paid out to the beneficiaries will be about 91% of all the tax savings that is being made due to the fund, so this is of course a win-win situation for all parts in the project.

You can't be over the age of 70 when the payment is due to be processed, that means if it takes 1 year from today for us to obtain the necessary number of beneficiaries you have to be under the age of 69 today. Hopefully it will not take that long. Children of any age can participate.

REQUIRED DOCUMENTATION FOR STARTING THE PROCESS OF PAYMENT TO THE BANKACCOUNTS:

1. Letter of Intent (LOI) from the principal (That explains that the client isn't involved in activities like moneylaundry, drugs, etc)

2. Client Information Sheet (CIS)

3. Colored passport copy of the beneficiary (PP), your signature on the copy.

4. Letter of Authorization to Verify and Authenticate.

5. Memorandum of Understanding (Non Circumvention - Non Disclosure, Working and Fee Protection Agreement) with Human Capital Insurance 25 (HCI25)

All of the documents mentioned above will be sent to you with clear description on how to fill them out. They will be sent in PDF. This will not have to be done until we have reached the necessary number of beneficiaries.

You will all get emails regarding this when the time comes.

CHANCES ARE GREAT THAT THE INVESTMENTS / PROJECTS / PLANS WILL BE CLOSED IF THE NECESSARY PAPERWORK ISN'T DONE. THIS IS THE NUMBER ONE REASON FOR FAILURE OF DIFFERENT PROJECTS.

All of these programs have several things in common. They all offer a low introductory investment amount. They either promise your principal is guaranteed, or they assure you your investment with them is safe with little or no risk. The scammers know that by keeping the dollar amount low, you will not go to the authorities to report them if they run with the money. The scammers also know that law enforcement is not going to conduct an investigation for such a small dollar amount of loss per person. While this is true, but if there are thousands in the same location who joined together it becomes real money in a hurry. But what they all do is promise you riches for a little bit of money invested in their program. It is the lure to get you to invest even more money as the program goes forward. Soon they have your life savings, you have taken a second out on your house to invest, you have borrowed from your 401(k), or you have charged your credit cards to the max to invest in the program. After all it is paying, and it is paying on time with a great rate of return. This is the 'gotcha' moment.

In the early stages of a scam, they do make payments. It is the means by which they lure others into joining in on the investment. As you begin receiving your payments, you are encouraged to invest your "return" back into the program so you can earn even more on your investment. When you see others doing the same thing, it encourages you to do the same. By this time you are hooked, and if you have not already done so, you now tell all your friends and family about this wonderful opportunity. So they too join and the process is repeated all over. What none of you realize is how close to the collapse you really are of this wonderful program when the membership explodes in growth.

All the programs mentioned above have collapsed except GPP and HCI, and we expect both to collapse soon. In fact we believe GPP has already pulled a runner (more on GPP in Chapter 13), and HCIs website is now offline. But there are a few things I want to point out about each of the programs to give you a better understanding of how they trick you into believing their story-line.

GNI tells you they are doing sports arbitrage betting, but then tell you it is not gambling. Their rational is because they claim there are no losing bets, it is not gambling. This is gambling no matter what they say, and you cannot always have winning bets with no losing ones. They claim they are trading, not betting. They also claimed your principal is 'guaranteed.' It collapsed, and people found out their principal was not 'guaranteed' as promised. It was merely words.

P-2-P also claimed your principal was guaranteed, and like GNI, when it folded more than 40,000 people in six continents learned this was not true. P-2-P claimed they had a system that was just like being on autopilot that made money no matter what happened in the markets. P-2-P was taking your investment money and piggy-backing on P-2-Ps trades. P-2-P also claimed they were not a HYIP program, but stated trading was done in FOREX, which is a HYIP product. They stated: *IMPORTANT NOTE: This is NOT a H.Y.I.P. site... We do NOT believe in them! You must stay away at all costs!*

TDU claimed that for a $30 investment you would receive $12,500 for your unit purchase. TDU never explained what a "unit" was, but no-one seemed to care what a unit was who joined. Now if you purchased more than one unit, and depending on how many units you purchased, instead of just receiving $12,500, your amount went up according to the number of units you purchased. If you purchased 2-3 units your payment increased to $17,500 per unit. If you purchased 4-5 units your payment increased to $22,500 per unit, and if you purchased 6 or more your payment was increased to $27,500 per unit. What was even more incredible to believe is that for every person you referred that bought one $30 unit, they would pay you $50 in a referral fee. Now stop and think about that for just a moment. You were receiving more money in your referral fee than the person who purchased the $30 unit. Now do you really believe they could pay $20 more for a referral fee than the cost of one $30 unit? Well, close to 10,000 people did, and the majority bought far more than one unit. After many missed payment deadlines, this collapsed after dragging on for 17 months, and everyone lost all their money.

Genius Funds offered you an initial investment for as low as $10 into one of their two market funds. The daily fund was promising a 1% - 1.9% rate of return, and the weekly fund was promising a 5.5% - 8.5% rate of return. For those investors who could invest a minimum of $300, they offered their High-Yield Deposit Account paying 14% monthly. Of course for those investors who could invest more, they had a program designed for you paying higher rates of return than you were currently obtaining from your investment portfolio. All secure of course as they had programs to alleviate the wild market swings. It too collapsed stealing millions.

The thing that was most interesting about the DR Fund is that it collapsed before it really got started. Even though it did, there were many people who thought this program would last a long time. The same story with all these programs, as people failed to see all the red flag warning signs waiving. Again they offered a low dollar investment amount to entice you into the program. One of the major discrepancies was the claim only 15 positions would be allowed per investor, and then they showed administrative costs for up to 20 positions. Even with this collapsing so quickly, millions were lost.

What I wanted you to take away from this chapter is that the program admin's are getting smarter by lowering the amount for people to invest in their programs, and many are claiming the principal is 'guaranteed.' If not 'guaranteed,' then to make you believe there is no way your money is at risk, or this is a Ponzi.

Let's Recap:

The admin of these scams know that people are desperate;

That people will invest if they believe their principal is guaranteed;

People will join a program and invest if the dollar amount to be invested is very low;

Once you are in the program, the admin knows he can get you to invest even more;

The admin convinces you to reinvest your return instead of cashing out;

The admin knows you will recruit for him to bring even more people into his program for his gain;

The more people he can convince to do this, the more money he will be able to steal when he runs; and

The admin will run, or get shut-down by the authorities. The only two options available to any scam investment program.

Next, I have asked Les Henderson, author of "Crimes of Persuasion-Schemes, Scams and Fraud" an expert on Prime Bank Notes/Letters of Credit to address this topic.

Prime Bank Notes/Letters Of Credit – They Do Exist, Don't They?

Private Bank Notes/Letters of Credit (PBNs/LCs, as they are usually referred to), are said to be notes from the worlds top 100 banks that can be bought at discount and then sold for a huge profit when they mature. Only one problem; they don't exist. Contrary to what you will be told, they are a myth.

The story line goes that these are instruments that only the super-wealthy have access to in the financial markets. They are hush-hush products, and the banks won't admit they exist because they don't want to share these with anyone but the super wealthy. You are also told that if you contact any banking agency, or major bank, they will all deny they exist because they don't want word getting out they exist so they can keep you from participating in them. They are purportedly safe investments because they are backed by a Letter of Credit.

Les Henderson, author of the book "Crimes of Persuasion-Schemes, Scams and Frauds," and his Crimes of Persuasion website explains how this scam works, and I quote:

"How Prime Bank Guarantee/Letters of Credit Scams Work:

They offer you extremely high yields in a relatively short period of time through access to "bank guarantees" which they say they can buy at a discount and sell shortly thereafter at an enormous premium.

You are told that institutions like pension funds stand ready to buy "Prime Bank letters of credit" from large banks, with purchases of over $100 million affording the highest return, but because regulatory restrictions prevent the banks from selling directly to institutional investors a middle man is required to handle the transaction at a contractually prearranged profit.

The big banks around the world supposedly lend each other money by issuing notes with face values of $100 million or more. These notes can be resold a number of times at a discount (profit) to other lenders so that the original issuer can reap a handsome profit in a relatively short time. The term of the notes vary from 30 days to a year or more.

As an insider they are able to buy below par at, say 77 cents then sell for 79 cents on a continuous basis. For example, if $10 million worth of "bank guarantees" can be sold at about a two percent profit on ten separate occasions, or "traunches," you will receive a 20% profit in about thirty days.

An Exclusive Club

They say that "the Rothchilds and the Rockefellers set up the process over fifty years ago during the creation of the Marshall Plan as a means of utilizing Eurodollars which were beginning to flow overseas, and to fund "off-the-balance-sheet" rebuilding projects in developing countries."

They further explain: "The prime banks have generally dealt only with the world's wealthiest, such as the Saudis or the top financiers on Wall Street, in London or Geneva but competition has opened it up." "Still, only big corporations, foreign banks and ultra-wealthy investors know about the process."

They divulge that a "Saudi oil sheik wants to invest seven billion dollars" and "the Onassis family wants to invest $250 million dollars" in this very offering which is "based on an arrangement among various governments to stabilize the Eurodollar money supply using a handful of picked traders."

You are told not to bother seeking professional advice because the information is reserved only for those who participate in the program which is 'by invitation only'. You are told that you are one of only a few people who will qualify in this undertaking along with "an elite group of investors with access to extremely valuable and highly confidential information."

The Magic of Pooling

The minimum investment can be as high as $10,000,000, either from an individual, or a group of individuals who pool their smaller investments. It's this pooling of investors' funds which gives you the resources to purchase "prime bank" financial instruments.

Brokers get involved to help small investors pool their money to build it up to the minimum $10 to $100 million. You are also told that potential annual profits of 100% or more are possible with little risk and you could yield up to five times your money in two months, with such returns guaranteed.

For Your Eyes Only

They convince you to transfer assets or borrow the money to invest in the program after signing special non-disclosure and non-circumvention agreements which prevent you from talking about the deal with anyone, including lawyers or financial advisors because you are joining "a privileged group getting in on a very exclusive investment which relies on secrecy."

All transactions are to be kept strictly confidential by all parties and for this reason no client references will be available. In an effort to lull you into inaction, they emphasize that the market for these instruments is so secret that the institutions involved and even regulatory agencies will deny the existence of the program if asked.

You risk being permanently expelled from participating in these transactions along with being hit with a massive bank-backed breach of contract lawsuit should you attempt to independently investigate the offering.

"Keep this information secret. If anyone finds out I am doing this for you, the deal is off."

You are also told not to phone the bank listed on the documents because they cannot acknowledge the existence of such an arrangement unless you are the principle investor ($10 million on deposit) and besides, the process is so restricted that even the low level staff, such as bank managers, wouldn't know about it even if you did ask.

He says that the returns offered are considerably higher than are available under normal market conditions and, therefore, if this activity was not kept secret it could not exist for the simple reason that it would make it very difficult for governments to fund treasury securities or for banks to offer conventional instruments such as CDs and GIC's paying far less.

"If it was widely known about, people wouldn't settle for much lower returns. They would seek out this instrument. So the only way it can be handled is on a very private basis where people make the application in highly structured ways and if allowed to participate they get access to a direct contract."

Proof of Authenticity

The notes are shown to be issued and guaranteed by large, well-known international banks like Barclays, Lloyds Bank, Chase Manhattan and Deutsche Bank.

When you ask why the banks offer the paper so cheaply they note that there are several factors involved such as:

- The banks are currently funding credit card receivables at 28% so 2% is nothing,
- The International Monetary Fund is funding covert development aid to African governments,
- Executives at the bank are taking part of the skim themselves and want it to continue,
- The money goes to finance international investments such as roads and health care facilities, and
- World bank loans to Third World countries get written off in the end.

They tell you that they have no interest in stealing your money because they make enough from the deal already and want to have you participate in the next program so you can both get rich together.

Many exotic sounding banking terms are used which are confusing to all but the professional banker or investor. Soon you feel too self-conscious and ignorant to ask further questions. As the investment appears to involve overly complex loan funding mechanisms this makes even a questionable investment appear worthwhile.

When you ask for references you are shown high-quality documents emanating from institutions such as the U.S. Federal Reserve, the IMF (International

Monetary Fund), the World Bank, the Bank of England and even the Queen of England to win your confidence but, with the secrecy provisions, there is no way to check their authenticity.

They even question "your" integrity when they suggest you might have to have a background check done by Scotland Yard or Interpol to ensure that your funds are not from money laundering or drug sources.

They may offer the return of your investment in "a year and a day" and produce complex forms required by the International Chamber of Commerce (ICC) under the specific guidelines known as ICC 500.

The U.S. government issued its first warning about prime bank note frauds in 1993, but the publication of the book *The Creature From Jekyll Island* in 1994 by G. Edward Griffin continues to fuel new investor interest in prime bank notes. The book, which promoters of prime bank notes urge skeptics to read, describes a labyrinth of secret transactions that enable the Federal Reserve system, governments and international banks to control the U.S. and world economies.

As Secure As They Come

You may be told that as an investor, and not a principle (you don't have $10 million), you either have no personal security or that there is no need to worry because every penny is fully secured by a Letter of Credit, a bank-endorsed guarantee or other guaranteed bank certificate backed by the world's top or "prime banks." The word prime is synonymous with the phrase "top fifty world banks" and is used to refer to financial institutions of high repute and financial soundness.

They could also say it is both risk-free and sanctioned by the International Monetary Fund, that it has an "IMF Number", an "IMF Country Registration Number," or an "IMF Approval Number for Projects."

The Charity Angle

You may be told that the profits are so vast that you can't expect to retain all the money because the Federal Reserve expects you to sponsor humanitarian projects in the Third World. They will often have set up the infrastructure and name for this benevolent organization which is simply another layer of deception to add complexity and an aura of respectability to the whole operation and to counterbalance any twinges of guilt you might have when feelings of greed pass over you.

You are then shown a full-colour glossy brochure complete with pictures of crying malnourished children, maps and graphs and are then asked to pick your favourite amongst such worthy objectives as irrigation projects, cornea transplants for the blind or Nicaraguan housing developments for the poor.

Save Taxes Too!

You are intrigued when told that it is possible for a shrewd investor to utilize a tax haven country, with their help, so that no tax need be paid on your phenomenal returns.

They encourage you to send your money to a foreign bank, where it is eventually transferred to an offshore account that is solely with in their control. Should you wish to make any trouble they will threaten to ruin your credit history with their massive, but non-existent, resources.

It Sounds Good

You are offered an investment in Global Investments Networks' "High Yield International Private Investment Program". The written materials state that the investment offers an excellent yield of 3% interest per month for a twelve-month period, with very little risk.

They include illustrations of the compounded return that can be achieved at this rate for an investment of $10,000 and multiples of $10,000. Your money is to be managed through a cooperative agreement between a program manager and a "licensed chartered bank."

The funds will be deposited into a "blocked account" at the bank. The funds are secured by a guarantee issued by a "Top Money Center Bank" and are to be used for trading bank debentures which are regulated by the International Chamber of Commerce. The materials characterize these programs as "highly privileged insider opportunities."

The materials do not identify the principals in Global Investments Network Ltd., their track record, the identity of the program manager, the bank where the funds will be deposited, the identity of the "guarantee" bank, what role or compensation Global is to receive, or what basis they have for the claim to be able to pay investors 3% per month.

The materials do include instructions on how to invest, a letter of intent and a private placement application, as well as a form to verify that you have not been convicted of a felony or involved in any white collar crimes, terrorist activities, money laundering or bank fraud.

These are to be completed by you and returned, together with proof of funds on deposit in a financial institution after which they promise to quickly relieve you of your money."

(http://www.crimes-of-persuasion.com/Crimes/InPerson/MajorPerson/prime_bank.htm),

Let's Recap:

Here's what you need to remember so you won't become a victim of this type of scam:

1. Prime Bank Notes/Letters of Credit are a MYTH. They do not exist.
2. There is no exclusive club of high net-worth individuals who trade in these Notes.
3. There is no "Pooling" of your funds with other high net-worth individuals. The only "pooling" going on is you and the others who fall for this scam.

4. The Charity is non-existent, or if it exists has no knowledge of this group and will never receive a dime. It is to make you think you and they are doing good works.
5. It is not a super secret world of trading that is only known to limited banks and people.
6. It is all a lie to separate you from your money, and you will never receive a payment; as there will always be an excuse as to why the payment has been delayed.
7. The SEC, FTC, FBI, DOJ, and the Secret Service all have warnings about the Prime Bank Note Scams on their websites.

Now that you know how this scam works, and that they are not real, you should not become a victim of this scam. Thanks Les for providing this valuable information.

I keep hearing about all these work-from-home opportunities out there, and I get lots of E-mails about them, but how do I know they are real? I have asked my good friend and expert, Paul Schlegel, from workathometruth.com (www.workathometruth.com), to discuss how you can tell the real work-from-home-opportunities from the scams.

Work From Home – Real Or Fake?

Paul Schlegel, Founder Of WorkAtHomeTruth And The Brutally Honest Truth About Working At Home

I'm always surprised to find that I have to educate people about home business and home job scams that come back year after year -- the types of scams that get shut down by the Federal Trade Commission time after time. And the type of scams that have generated enormous numbers of complaints year after year.

But scam artists love a proven "scam model" and they definitely live – and scam – by the motto, "If it ain't broke, don't fix it!"

I've helped thousands of people avoid work at home scams over the years at my WorkAtHomeTruth.com website and I think I can help you, too. You may have to learn some new things, forget some old myths, and accept that in many cases the bad guys can't be stopped, but only avoided.

And that's what I want to help you to do – avoid the bad guys, avoid work at home scams, and if you want, learn the right way to find legitimate home jobs, freelance work from home, and home businesses.

Let's start by shaking up things a little bit and possibly exploding your idea of how to use the BBB in your work at home quest...

The Right Way To Use The BBB In Your Work At Home Quest

Most people don't use the Better Business Bureau site the right way – especially when it comes to using it to research companies in their "work at home" quest. The Better Business Bureau (the BBB) is a bit of a strange animal when it comes to evaluating companies in the work at home arena.

Here are a few of the things you need to keep in mind if you are going to use the BBB as part of your due diligence in finding a legitimate work at home opportunity.

1. The BBB often gives a company an F rating merely of "concerns with the industry in which a business operates." In other words the BBB may know nothing at all about a company and still give it an F rating.
2. The BBB often lumps "home job" companies and "home business" companies under the same "work at home" category. But as you'll soon learn, for purposes of due diligence you have to treat a home job search and home business search completely differently.
3. As the BBB itself notes, you have to "take into account the company's size and volume of transactions, and understand that the nature of complaints and a firm's responses to them are often more important than the number of complaints."

I'll be covering the first two points in other sections. But for now let's take a look at that last caveat which comes from the BBB itself:

"When considering complaint information, please take into account the company's size and volume of transactions, and understand that the nature of complaints and a firm's responses to them are often more important than the number of complaints."

In other words, all things being equal you should be more concerned about a company with 50 complaints that does 1,000 transactions per month than a company with 500 complaints that does 1,000,000 transactions per month.

However, for various reasons it's not always possible to know the volume of transactions a company actually does. That's why it's usually more important to look at the "nature of the complaints". In other words if you see that 95% of the complaints against a company are similar in nature– say "failure to honor their refund policy" that's definitely something to pay attention to and to consider as a red-flag.

What Does "Work At Home" Actually Mean?

As mentioned previously, the BBB often lumps "home job" companies and "home business" companies under the same "work at home" category. So what does "work at home" actually mean – and why is it important to know?

It's important to understand the different categories of "working at home" because your strategy for avoiding scams and performing due diligence isn't the same for each type of "work at home" category.

The main work at home categories are as follows:

Home jobs – These are like any other employer/employee type job, pay, benefits, and perks vary from company to company. Although they do exist, they actually are the smallest percentage of total legitimate work at home opportunities.

Freelance work from home – A freelancer or (freelance worker) is self-employed and is considered an "independent contractor" and is responsible for paying their own benefits and taxes. Freelance work is available in just about any field you can imagine.

Home business opportunities – are typically based on a blueprint or step-by-step plan. Revenue is usually generated through product sales, commissions, or advertising revenue.

Work at home scams – Whether it's fair or not, the largest and most popular work at home programs are almost always a scam. Day after day, these scammers are getting smarter and more sophisticated. The bad news is work at home scams force most people to give up the idea of working from home. After getting scammed and disappointed time after time, many just assume all work at home opportunities are scams.

You don't have to be one of those people who give up your dream of working at home. When you understand the main categories of working at home, let's take a look at how you can avoid work at home scams and find legitimate work at home opportunities.

First, you need to approach each type of work at home opportunity a bit differently. You especially need to separate how you do your due diligence on "telecommuting work" and how you do your due diligence when evaluating "home businesses". [The next two sections will show you how to do both.

But first let me correct one of the biggest mistakes I hear people making when they are searching for telecommuting or freelance work. And that mistake is the misuse of the "never pay for a job" red-flag.

- **What "Never Pay For A Job" Really Means**

While "never paying for a job" is a good and important rule, it seems to be completely misunderstood by a large number of people.

What "never pay for a job" means, of course, is that you shouldn't pay for someone to hire you to do work for them him or her or to show that "you are serious".

But some things that "never pay for a job" does NOT mean are:

1. "Never pay for a job" does NOT mean never pay for a legitimate database of potential freelance and telecommuting work. There are, in fact, legitimate databases of potential telecommuting (home job) positions. You are NOT paying for a job in those cases. You are paying for experts to screen out scams, save you time, and bring you legitimate potential freelance and telecommuting opportunities.
2. "Never pay for a job" does NOT mean that you should never pay for home business training. I'm not even sure how people get this idea into their mind, because as explained earlier a home business is completely different from a home job or freelance work.
3. "Never pay for a job" does NOT mean that you should never pay for certain types of fees. Although you normally should not pay any sort of fees, there are a handful of legitimate companies that offer freelance work that will require you to pay for background checks, credit checks. For example, LiveOps is a legitimate outsourcing call center solution that uses work at home agents and currently charges a $30.00 [fee for a credit and background check. However, that being said, for most companies you should still be very cautious if they try to charge you some sort of fee.

With that out of the way, let's look at important rules to follow when searching for home jobs and freelance work.

Rules To Follow And Warnings When Searching For Home Jobs And Freelance Work

When searching and applying for telecommuting positions (home jobs or freelance work) you should use the following precautions:

Rule #1: Never pay to apply for a job or to show "you're serious".

[Important Note: as covered previously, this is different from paying for a legitimate home job or freelance work database that can be OK (see the following explanation for even more details)...

Do you **need** to pay for a home job or freelance work database? No. But if you are a person who is **new** to searching for home jobs or freelance work or has searched without success, a paid database can play several important roles:

1. It can free up the time you spend on searching for home jobs and/or freelance work
2. It can show you types of work that you have skills for that you may never hear of otherwise.
3. It can show you what real home job and freelance work listings look like. This can be a huge help to prevent you from falling for scams.
4. It can help you find much better words to use when doing your own job searches.

In other words, besides helping you **find** a home job, a legitimate home job and freelance work database can be an amazing educational tool to help you become a smart searcher of home jobs and freelance work.

Legitimate home job and freelance work databases use experienced researchers to find their positions. So checking their listings against the types you find on your own can be a huge eye-opener. The value of this should not be underestimated.

It bears repeating that there's a major difference between paying for a job (Not OK) and paying to access a legitimate database of job listings or freelance work listings (OK).

Be cautious about calling unfamiliar area codes

Some international pay-per-call area codes look like legitimate U.S. area codes and employment scammers will use that to get you to call a number that you unwittingly get charged for.

Before you return a phone call from an employer with an unfamiliar area code you might check it against this list of Caribbean area codes. Calling phone numbers with certain area codes might be linked to pay-per-call services with large up-front fees.

You can check what geographic area an area code belongs to at http://www.fonefinder.net/. You can also check your telephone directory or call the operator to determine if the area code is for a domestic or international location before calling.

Never allow a company to deposit a check into your account to "test or process the check".

In this scheme, generally the scammer will tell you to deposit the check, keep a portion for your services, and then wire the rest back.

You'll soon discover they sent you a fake check, the check will bounce, and you'll be stuck responsible for the full amount, including the money you sent back to the scammer.

Don't give a company your checking account information or social security number until you're comfortable with them.

A major source of fraud today is called "demand draft" fraud.

Here's how it works:

Once you provide the account information, a criminal creates a "demand draft" (i.e. a remotely created check that doesn't require a signature) and withdraw funds from your account -- often without your permission.

They get away with it because demand drafts generally only require the customers typewritten checking account number, a notation that the customer authorized the draft and/or a statement such as the statement "No signature required," "Authorization on file," "Signature on file," or words similar to that effect.

Use *extreme caution* if you click on advertising at even the most legitimate sites.

Many of the best sites don't have much control over many of the ads that display on their sites. Even when the site seems legitimate, it doesn't mean the ads lead to legitimate products and services, too.

Limit the amount of personal information you give when first applying for a job

If you know that a job is obviously legitimate, then this wouldn't apply. However, if you're unsure at all, then you should only include your first name and e-mail address. Once you become more familiar and comfortable with the company you can reveal further information.

Next let's move onto rules to follow when looking for and evaluating home businesses and home business training. Unfortunately, the rules for evaluating home businesses and home business training aren't nearly as clear-cut as those you use for searching for home job and freelance work. Looking for legitimate home businesses and home business training is a bit like entering an area of the "wild west" where anything goes and even the sheriff doesn't always understand the "rules of the game".

Rules To Follow And   Warnings When Searching For And Evaluating Home Businesses

Although there is plenty of good information about how to research business opportunities that fall under business opportunity disclosure rules, when it comes to looking for less expensive home business opportunities and home business training it's a bit like entering an area of the "wild west" where anything goes and even the sheriff doesn't always understand the "rules of the game".

If you are researching a higher priced business opportunity or a franchise, there is already plenty of good information at places like the Federal Trade Commission. The information at:

http://www.ftc.gov/bcp/menus/business/franchise.shtm would be the first stop I recommend, followed by http://www.franchise-info.ca/.

But when it comes to looking for low-cost home business opportunities and home business training many of the FTC due diligence rules don't apply and you will mainly need to identifying red flags. Here are the big ones (in no particular order). None of the following are absolute proof that a home business opportunity is a scam, but they can be considered "indicators" (red-flags). In other words, the more of them you find, the less likely you are to be dealing with a legitimate home business or legitimate home business training.

Red flag #1) Home businesses or home business training that promise that anyone can make money fast or make money while they he or she sleep

While it's true that you can eventually "make money fast" or "while you sleep" in a home business, it is NOT true that you can do it right off the bat. You have to put in real work and build up your business assets first. E.g., sure you can make money fast if you have a list of 20,000 email subscribers you can email a promotion to – and hey, they might even buy while you're sleeping. What the home business hucksters fail to mention is the amount of time and hard work it will take you to develop and build that email list. The same is true with any asset of real long-term value.

Red flag #2) the type of opportunity being offered

Often there are legitimate versions of the types of business opportunity fraud that scammers perpetrate, which is part of what helps scammers effectively perpetrate these scams. Business opportunity scams that con artists use time and time again are:

- 900 Numbers – besides a large majority of the "900 number business opportunities" being outright scams another problem with 900 phone numbers business opportunities these days is that consumers can le-gally decline to pay for a 900 number Call. Under FCC regulations, the phone company cannot disconnect a customer's regular local or long-distance service if they don't pay a

- 900 number charge. However, they could be blocked from making future calls to 900 phone numbers if they don't pay legitimate 900 number charges.
- Cash Gifting – claims to be legal, but isn't
- Chain Letters – claim to be legal, but aren't.
- Coupon Businesses – "cents off" and "coupon clipping" clipping scams.
- Display Racks
- Government Grants – often make it appear that you "qualify for" or are "guaranteed" a grant, which is impossible for them to know. Or they will claim to tell you where to find "small business grants" that essentially don't exist.
- Greeting Card business opportunities
- Home Business Kits – typically with a small initial "trial fee".
- HUD Refund Tracers/Processors
- Invention Promotion Companies - They insist on advance payment - yet also insist that they make their money from royalties. Reputable firms usually work on a contingency basis, and there is no real reason the company in question shouldn't be able to work this way.
- Medical Billing – often involves high pressure sales tactics to get you to buy expensive medical billing software by salespeople who claim they will help you succeed. Once they have your money, the help that was promised is nowhere to be found.
- Modeling Agencies – often are just a way to get money out of you by claiming that you need to pay for photo shoots, screen tests, or classes
- Turnkey Websites – typically come with a "coach" who is actually a salesperson to try get you to buy very expensive and worthless advertising
- Unclaimed money recovery scams – charge you for information freely and easily available at http://www.missingmoney.com or http://www.unclaimed.org
- Vending Machine scams

Red flag #3) No contact information on the company's website – or at least in the terms and conditions page of the company website.

Red flag #4) The company is using a non-clickable trust seal or security seal on their website.

When security seals and trust seals are used on a website, they are supposed to be clickable so that you can verify their legitimacy through the seal provider's 3rd-party database. Home business scam sites often will fake many of the more popular security and trust seals – including, but not the BBB, TRUSTE, McAfee Secure, Verisign, Trust Guard, and COMODO

Red flag #5) The company operates out of Cypress, Guatemala, or Nevis, St. Kitts – especially if the terms state that the governing law is in one of those countries.

The intent behind this that if a person has a dispute with the company he or she have to go to Cyprus to settle it. There are ways around it in certain circumstances, but it should be considered   a red-flag.

Red flag #6) The company operates out of Utah, Arizona, or Nevada

Like it or not, a large number of popular U.S. based home business scams originate out of Utah, Arizona, and Nevada.

Red flag #7) The company uses fake testimonials or stock photos with testimonials

Online you can use reverse image lookup search engines like http://www.tineye.com to determine if a picture that goes with a testimonial is a stock photo or is used on other sites. You can use http://www.copyscape.com to try to find the same testimonial across different websites.

Red flag #8) How the home business is advertised online

How a home business is advertised online can tell you much about how likely it is to be legitimate or not. Currently two extremely popular ways of marketing questionable home businesses and downright scams are through fake news sites and fake blogs. Even if one of these types of sites uses an "Advertorial" disclaimer, you should consider this type of advertising a red flag.

Most of these fake news sites and fake blogs can easily be identified   by looking for one or more of the following:

- An "Advertorial" disclaimer
- A comments section stating something like "comments are closed due to spam"
- Taking a paragraph of information from the site and running it through http://www.copyscape.com

Red flag #9) How the home business is advertised offline

If a home business or home business training is advertised in newspaper classified advertising, or in popular "Income Opportunity" or "Business Opportunity" magazines, you should consider this type of advertising a red flag.

Red flag #10) Use of talking actors on an online sales page

A large number of questionable home business opportunities or outright scams have started using talking actors on their sales page. You can check places like http://www.livefaceonweb.com , http://www.liveonpage.com, http://www.ispeakvideo.com, http://www.myvirtualspokesperson.com and other "virtual spokesperson" sites to see if the person talking on the screen to you is actually who they he or she claims to be.

Red flag #11) Fake review sites

Here are a few red-flags and warning signs to look out for when reading home business reviews

The main Red-flag/Warning: The home based income opportunity recommended is owned by the person reviewing the opportunity – but the reviewer doesn't TELL you that.

I have no problem with a reviewer recommending his or her own home business income opportunity – as long as they tell you that they are the owner/creator of that home business income opportunity.

Some typical elements for Red-flag/Warning #1 are shown in the diagram below:

Fake Home Business Reviews

The easy red-flags for almost anyone to spot fake home business reviews are the following:

1. Fake Home Business Review Award Site (I've NEVER seen a real one of these)
2. Fake Seals Of Approval (Often will say something like "Certified Scam-Free" or will be made to sound like a legitimate seal of approval. E.g., "Consumer Reporting Agency" instead of "Consumer Reports"
3. A request for donations (this is done to make you believe the site is a nonprofit site)
4. All of the products recommended in the home business review are owned by the reviewer (this red-flag is not as easy to spot for most people as the other 3 – if you aren't sure about an opportunity feel free to contact me at WorkAtHomeTruth.com and ask me about it)

Red flag #12) Fake seals of approval, fake trust seals, and fake security seals

If you see a seal of approval, trust seal, or security seal you've never heard of before on a sales page for a home business opportunity, there's a good chance that the seal is fake. Sometimes the fake seals will create a fake seal "database" to make you think the seal is legitimate because it is "clickable" and goes to a database at another site. If you can't find a company that you already know is legitimate using the seal, be extremely skeptical of the validity of the seal.

Red flag #13) Non-clickable "As Seen On" logos

Home business opportunity sales page seem to love using logos claiming that they were seen in well-known places like CNN, MSNBC, ABC, USAToday, Entrepreneur, etc.

Legitimate sites typically make these seals clickable to the story where their company was referenced.

Red flag #14) Video testimonials that sound scripted

If you think that a video testimonial on a website sounds like it's being performed   by a paid actor. Guess what? It probably is!

Paying actors to do video testimonials for home business products is shockingly rampant. And   sadly, there appear to be plenty of people eager to make a buck providing them.

Here is a real example I found of someone paying for a video testimonial just by taking 30 seconds to search a popular freelance site:

"What I Need: I need a total of 4 video testimunials both male and female. These testimonials will be approximately 30 seconds to a minute each. I need 4 testimonials all together. The testimonials have to look real of course. I will provide you with scripts for all four of the testimonials, you don't have to memorize the entire script. The goal is to get the basic concept down, use any names in the script and stay on track about the products talked about."

One Caveat About Home Business Opportunities, Home Business Training And "Red Flags"

One caveat is that many times the sales page for a legitimate home business opportunity or home business training will look like and be hyped- up like one for a scam product. The solution? Use your head and common sense. It's also a smart idea to network and find people you trust that you can "hang out" with virtually or physically to share your experiences of what's working for you and what isn't and to hone your B.S. detection skills.

Still, the more red-flags you identify with a home business opportunity, the less likely it is to be legitimate.

How And Where To File Complaints Against Work At Home Scams

If you are the victim of a work at home scam, whether it's a home job scam, freelance work scam, or home business scam and wish to help law enforcement and other consumers, you can file complaints at the following places:

- The Federal Trade Commission at
- https://www.ftccomplaintassistant.gov/
- The Internet Crime Complaint Center at http://www.ic3.gov
- Your county or state consumer protection agency. Check the blue pages of the phone book under county and state government or you can look for them at http://www.consumeraction.gov/state.shtml
- The state attorney general's office in the state where you live and in the state where the business opportunity promoter is based. You can find the information you need at
- http://www.naag.org/current-attorneys-general.php
- The Better Business Bureau in your area and the area where the promoter is based. Go to http://complaint.bbb.org to file your complaint. Sometimes the BBB can help you resolve your complaint.

Note, the federal and state government agencies will NOT typically put out warnings because doing so could jeopardize their case before they have time to collect evidence. However, the BBB will issue warnings and the FTC goes through their documentation in case they need extrinsic evidence to make a judgment on matters of deception.

How To Get Your Money Back From Scammers

If you paid with a credit card, then you will want to file a dispute with your credit card company. You can usually find out how to file a dispute with your credit card company by looking on the back of your monthly statement. Usually your credit card company will require that you've tried to work out a dispute directly with the merchant. If the BBB has already put out a warning about a company you are filing a dispute against, you may want to point them to the BBB warning.

If you paid with a debit card, you will need to contact your bank about the dispute procedure to follow. There is also good information about how to work with your banks and credit card companies at:

HelpWithMyBank.gov.

Resources:

Home Job & Freelance Work Websites

- *IveTriedThat.com* – offers a free, 45 page guide that will show you where and how to find real work at home jobs, and freelance work.
- These are jobs that will PAY you to work. You will never have to pay for anything.
- *RatRaceRebellion.com* - Launched the pioneering virtual-careers training company, Staffcentrix in 1999. They post free job leads and resources at the RatRaceRebellion.com site. Founder, Chris Durst appears regularly on CNN as an Internet Fraud and Safety Expert.
- *TelCoa.org* – The Telework Coalition. Enables and supports the advancement of virtual, mobile, and distributed work through research, education, technology, and legislation
- *The International Virtual Assistants Association (IVAA)* - The International Virtual Assistants Association (IVAA) is a nonprofit organization dedicated to the professional education and development of members of the Virtual Assistance profession.
- *MysteryShop.org* – The Mystery Shopping Providing Association. This is the correct place to get information about mystery shopping opportunities.
- *FlexJobs.com* – has a trained staff of real people (and VERY knowledgeable people at that!) scour thousands of online resources for jobs - such as individual employer websites, industry blogs, reliable public job boards, and online newspaper classifieds -- for all of the most current postings that involve some level of telecommuting and online work.
- *HomeJobStop.com* – The Homejobstop Job Bank is an active job board specializing in home jobs and freelance work listings.
- *Wahm.com* – has a good forum where you can often get feedback from people about specific companies
- *WorkAtHomeTruth.com* – I have a telecommuting tool to help you search for legitimate home jobs and freelance work at http://www.workathometruth.com/TelecommutingTool.php

Home Business Resources

- WorkAtHomeTruth.com – This is my site where I help people find legitimate home businesses and also do extensive analysis of home business scams. There is a huge and evergrowing section of websites to avoid in the "Not Recommended" section at http://www.workathometruth.com/not-recommended/
- SparkPlugging.com – provides extensive information and resources for home-based entrepreneurs and those who want to become home-based entrepreneurs.
- Business.gov – this is an extremely helpful government site to help you understand licensing requirements, etc. for your home business. There is also a forum at http://community.business.gov
- SBA.gov – The Small Business Association

Work At Home Scam Educational Resources

- FakeChecks.org - Created by the National Consumers League (NCL), the nation's oldest nonprofit consumer organization, as a central source of information and advice about fake check scams.
- OnGuardOnline.gov – provides practical tips from the federal government and the technology industry to help you be on guard against Internet fraud, secure your computer, and protect your personal information.
- FraudWatchInternational.com – Specializes Phishing Fraud prevention. Includes free alert service.
- Consumer Action Handbook at ConsumerAction.gov
- FTC.gov – The Federal Trade Commission's Bureau Of Consumer Protection at http://www.ftc.gov/bcp/index.shtml
- RealScam.com – Fraud fighting forum
- WorkAtHomeTruth.com – especially the "Not Recommended" section at http://www.workathometruth.com/not-recommended/

Thanks Paul for all that useful information, and letting people know what action they need to take, and where to file a complaint when they have been scammed.

The next topic that is making a huge comeback on the Internet and through E-mail are the Cash Gifting Schemes. They make a lot of claims about being legal and not a pyramid, but is this really true? So just what is Cash Gifting, is it legal or illegal, and who's telling the truth?

Cash Gifting – Legal Or Illegal?

The latest scam targeting the Christian Community is the Cash Gifting Scheme. There are many different forms that Cash Gifting can take, but they all have the same thing in common…they are all illegal regardless of their format. Here is one format of cash gifting demonstrating what they claim, how the cash gifting promoters claim they work, and why they are illegal.

Here's what they claim:

What is private cash gifting?

Private gifting is a concept embraced by private groups of individuals and has been in existence for many years. Our private activity does not involve network marketing, multi-level marketing, or a business or commercial activity. There are no business transactions, investments and/or securities involved in this activity. There is no business or company name or location and there are no directors, officers, shareholders or principals. **Individuals simply support each other in a team concept and help change lives.**

The concept of private gifting is based upon the fact that American citizens have the Constitutional right to gift property, cash and other assets, and are subject to the rules and regulations established by the laws. The U.S. gifting rules are found in the IRS Tax Code, Title 26, Sections 2501-2504 and 2511.

The law states that one or more individuals can give a gift to another individual of up to $13,000 each per calendar year without any tax liability to either the giver or receiver of the gift, because the tax on the gift has already been paid. **WE ARE NOT GIVING TAX ADVICE. Tax evasion is illegal. Please consult a local CPA regarding whether your gifts are taxable.**

Is this a pyramid?

Not at all. A pyramid is associated with an investment scheme, a company or a business. We are not a company, just a private sharing club. We have zero sales quotas, we do not sell positions. Everyone gives the same gifts, works together in a team and has the potential of receiving the same gifts.

How did this concept begin?

Giving private gifts to one another is an expression of kindness, which has been going on for centuries. Governments have allowed its practice for individuals to share their wealth with families, friends and others. It has been a means of helping and blessing others on special occasions or when the need arises. Many cultures gift as a matter of course. Asian, Jewish and South American communities gift individuals within their culture on a regular basis so that they may start a business or buy a home. They in turn gift someone else to help enhance their lives. Habitat for Humanity is a great example of private gifting. Everyone participates with their time, their talents and materials to build a home for someone else. Some participate with a hammer, some with nails, some with food and others with the monetary gifts to purchase the supplies, but all create a team that works together to bless someone's life.

How does Cash Gifting work?

This activity is offered only by means of an exclusive one-to-one invitation. When someone accepts the invitation, they can move through a natural progression from the giving to the receiving stages of the activity. In this activity, there is no fixed hierarchy of individuals who have an advantageous position or unfair advantage over new participants.

Who can participate?

This is a private sharing group, and is offered only through an exclusive one-on-one invitation to individuals over 18 years of age who live in the United States. You are invited to learn more about our activity and become part of something extraordinary.

Anyone can do this. Whether you are currently employed part-time or full-time, unemployed, retired, disabled, a student, single parent or a busy housewife. All you have to do is be willing to give!

Is this a company?

There isn't a company. We are a team of individuals and we give "Gifts" to one another. We are not a business or an investment. A company can't withhold or misplace our gift. We are totally in control and in charge of our own gifts and give directly one to another.

Do I Need a Computer to Participate?

You will need to check your Eagles Den online several times each week. For those who don't have a computer, consider having a family member, friend, or Inviter, with a computer, help you get started. Please be sure it is someone you know, love and trust! In most areas, public libraries have Internet ready computers available to the public and staff who will teach you the basics of how to use them.

How can you give to a stranger?

How many times have you given to United Way, the Salvation Army and other charities? You don't know who got the gift, what stranger. The only difference here is that this person will start out as a stranger, but you will get to know them as part of the team, work with them and perhaps develop new friendships. We all have met some of the most wonderful people and have made a lot of new friends across the country and the world. These people are giving, they like team dynamics - they are people we want to meet and befriend.

Why would I want to participate?

"Gifting" has changed countless lives for the better. People who were about to lose their cars and homes have been saved from financial ruin, college education's have been made possible, and nearly forgotten dreams have come true, all from participation in "Gifting".

Is Cash Gifting Legal?

This is probably the number one question that pops up when people start to see the lucrative potential with this kind of activity, and it's certainly the first thing that we wanted to know too... after all, we have no interest in getting into any type of legal hot water, and we're sure you don't either, so here's what we found out. In researching this activity, it's important to keep in mind that there's no book out there that tells you what is legal in our society, only what is not legal. In the United States we have the Preamble, the Constitution and the Bill of Rights to protect a private citizen's rights to earn, pay taxes and give away property and cash as long as it's done according to the laws and codes of this country. The U.S. gifting rules are found in the IRS Tax Code, Title 26, Sections 2501-2504 and 2511. "Click here" for this document. In 2009 in the United States of America, the law states that one or more individuals can give a cash gift to another individual of up to $13,000 each per calendar year without any tax liability to either the giver or receiver of the gift, because the tax on the gift has already been paid. We also found that most well organized Cash Gifting programs require each participant to use some form of a Gifting Statement and/or Non-Solicitation form, which when signed, become binding agreements between two private individuals. These forms are used, it's said, to ensure the longevity and legality of a gifting program. So giving a gift of cash to someone, be it a friend, family member or a stranger is legal according to IRS code.

Now that you have seen what they claim, here is how the program works:

IMPORTANT INSTRUCTIONS ON HOW TO SEND YOUR GIFTS

1. Your gifts should be sent NO LATER than 24 hours after you receive the names of the (3) people you will be gifting on EACH LEVEL!

2. All gifts must be in cash, US Currency. No Money Orders, Cashier's Checks, personal checks, and so on.

3. Login to your website and in your back-office you will see the names of (3) people you are sending gifts. You will see their Name (Username), Phone Number, and Email Address.

4. Contact the people you are sending gifts and make sure you have their mailing address correct. For example, some people use different addresses for USPS and FedEx, so verify the correct address where to send your gift. Also, someone may be out of town for a week or two and want you to send their gift to their current location. In short, with every gift you send, always contact the person first for the current correct address. As soon as you have sent your gift, send an email letting the person receiving your gift know that it is on the way AND how it was sent (e.g., USPS, Priority Mail, FedEx, UPS, etc.), including the TRACKING NUMBER if it was sent by private courier.

Under no circumstances are you to send a gift to any person other than the (3) individuals who are listed in your back-office!

5. To electronically send the Gifting Statement & Non-Solicitation Form, login to your website and click on "Gifting Forms." In the box next to "Recipient's Username," type in the person's Username and click on "Submit." Fill in the form with the amount of your gift and type your name next to "Signature" at the bottom and click on "Send Now."

6. When sending anything by either USPS or private courier (e.g., FedEx, UPS, DHL, etc.), powerful scanners look into that envelope to make sure there is no contraband in the envelope and USPS and UPS have restrictions against sending cash. So, to prevent any problems with your sending cash gifts, follow these procedures to the letter.

If you do not follow these procedures, you will jeopardize the safety and longevity of the activity, so please be mindful of them:

1. Take the cash and wrap it in black paper.

2. Write a brief note on a regular, 8 1/2 by 11, white sheet of paper, such as: Hi Bill, Nice chatting with you! I am sending you this little gift of ($Amt.) to cheer your day and say thanks for your friendship. Have a nice day, (Your Name & Username). Fold that paper in three and put the black paper inside it.

3. Take that folded white sheet of paper and fold a sheet of black construction paper (purchased at any Art Supply Store or Office Supply Store, such as Staples, Office Depot, or Office Max) around it.

4. Put the folded sheet of black construction paper in a #10 SECURITY ENVELOPE, address the TO and FROM on the envelope, put a stamp on it, and put it in the mail.

5. When sending larger gifts by private courier (e.g., FedEx, UPS, DHL, etc.), do Steps 1 through 4, above, and put the smaller envelope in a manila folder (cut off the tab at the top part so it fits in a Priority Mail or private courier envelope) or old magazine (so it doesn't bounce around), and put it in the larger courier envelope.

6. It is very important that your small envelope containing the cash is addressed (To and From), sealed, and stamped. This is in case the larger, courier envelope should be in an accident, damaged and opened, and your smaller envelope with the cash falling out- you and your cash are protected because it is against the law to open an addressed, sealed, stamped envelope; it must be put in the mail right away and sent back on its way.

7. Your first few levels of gifts (Steps 1-3) can be sent via the Postal Service (USPS). DO NOT use a Delivery Confirmation Form! This will SLOW down your delivery and you need the gift to arrive as quickly as possible.

8. Beginning with Step 4 gifts ($100), you MUST send these using a private courier (e.g., FedEx, UPS, DHL, etc.) using TRACKING NUMBERS. DO NOT indicate in any way that there is "cash" in the envelope, for your own safety and protection. We recommend you send it Overnight Delivery. If it is okay with the person you are sending the gift, you can send it without having a "Signature Required." Some people are not home during the day to give a signature and do not mind having the envelope left at their door- it is entirely up to them, so please respect their wishes.

If the receiver of the gift requests that the courier envelope be left at their door, without "Signature Required," then the sender of the gift cannot be held responsible, as long as the Tracking Number confirms delivery.

9. For an easier and less expensive (only $1.00) gift-sending method, if both you and the person you are sending the gift have purchased the VISA Gold Debit Card (and you have it loaded with enough cash), you may send your gift from your card to their card. Could not get any easier!

10. As soon as you receive a gift from someone, IMMEDIATELY login to your website and under "Incoming Gifts," to the right of that person's name, click on "Confirm." It is imperative that you do this right away each time you receive a gift.

Many of the Cash Gifting programs require you to complete their Cash Gifting Forms. They may look like these, or may have other characteristics not listed here:

NON SOLICITATION

Private and Confidential

To:_____

Date:____/_____/_____

(Persons name you are requesting information from)

Dear Sir or Madam:

I, the undersigned, hereby confirm with full personal and legal responsibility, that I have requested this information of my own free will and accord, and that I am not seeking investment opportunities.

I hereby affirm that the information that I am requesting is about a private gifting activity.

I hereby confirm that neither you nor anyone on your behalf or anyone else associated with your activity has solicited me in any way. All parties state as truth that they are not employees or officials in or of any agency, and are not a member of the media whose purpose is to collect information for defamation or prosecution. All parties agree that falsification of this criteria entitles the party defrauded thereby is entitled to $100,000.00 (U.S.) for violation of rights against forced association.

Any documents or information received by me will not be construed as solicitation in any way whatsoever. I further affirm that I have been told that the nature of these activities is that of charity and I affirm that my involvement with gifting is solely a voluntary act of my own accord. I also understand that should I get involved with gifting that my gift will be just that, a gift, and it is nothing to which I may lay claim in the future; it is a gift. It is agreed that a fax copy will be considered legal and enforceable as an original.

Sincerely yours,

_____

Signature

_____

Print Name

Address, City, State, Zip Code

Gifting Statement

Private and Confidential

I,_____, do hereby declare under penalties of perjury that the following statements are true and correct to the very best of my knowledge. Any and all property of any nature that I transfer from my ownership and possession to the recipient of my gift is intended as a gift and not as an investment. I have not been sold anything, and I have not been offered any opportunity to do so.

I have been told not to expect any return of any nature, and I have received no license or privilege of soliciting or recruiting other parties. I will not at any time ask for this gift to be returned to me and with this statement, I waive any and all my rights to civil or criminal remedies against the recipient of my gift.

I perceive no agreement between myself and the recipient of my gift, and I expect no profit, benefit, or opportunity of any nature in consideration of the property that I have transferred as a gift. I believe that I am totally within the law, as it pertains to my activities herein described.

My intent is to give a gift of $_____to_____ as an individual. I do not intend the gift as an investment, nor as a payment for which I am owed anything of value; furthermore, I acknowledge that my gift does not entitle me to any future opportunity or benefit of any nature. I understand only gifts may be offered to a recipient and that no property may be offered with the intent of its owner suggesting a future return, or opportunity be obtained or secured by virtue of his/her having transferred said gift to another individual.

I have agreed under this gift statement to not reassert any right to the property that I now give freely as a gift to another individual. I am a fully informed and consenting adult and I have not been misled in anyway.

I do hereby declare that the foregoing statement is true and correct, and is binding upon me to the full extent expressed herein.

Executed this _____ day of _____, _____

SIGNATURE _____

Print Name_____

_____

ADDRESS, CITY, STATE, ZIP

* By participating in this activity you have in no way purchased a "position" or "spot". You have not purchased the right to make money or proceeds and you have in no way purchased the right to benefit from gifting. It simply means that you have given a gift and the participation with this activity is logged and recorded.

What you must remember about Cash Gifting programs is that some of what they say is the truth, but they conveniently omit information that contradicts what they claim, twist the truth, or make references that have nothing to do with Cash Gifting but designed to fool you into believing it is all legal.

Now you have seen what one type of cash gifting looks like, what they claim and how it works; now let's discuss what is the truth and what is omitted/twisted, which makes Cash Gifting Illegal in spite of what they claim:

What is private cash gifting?

Private gifting is a concept embraced by private groups of individuals and has been in existence for many years. Our private activity does not involve network marketing, multi-level marketing, or a business or commercial activity. There are no business transactions, investments and/or securities involved in this activity. There is no business or company name or location and there are no directors, officers, shareholders or principals. Individuals simply support each other in a team concept and help change lives.

While the majority of this statement is true, there are people behind these programs that make 85% of the money in these cash gifting schemes.

The concept of private gifting is based upon the fact that American citizens have the Constitutional right to gift property, cash and other assets, and are subject to the rules and regulations established by the laws. The U.S. gifting rules are found in the IRS Tax Code, Title 26, Sections 2501-2504 and 2511.

The law states that one or more individuals can give a gift to another individual of up to $13,000 each per calendar year without any tax liability to either the giver or receiver of the gift, because the tax on the gift has already been paid. WE ARE NOT GIVING TAX ADVICE. Tax evasion is illegal. Please consult a local CPA regarding whether your gifts are taxable.

What they have said here is true, but only up to a point. What they conveniently omitted telling you is what the IRS Code says in regard to your gift. The Code specifically states, and I quote: "your gifts must be given WITH ABSOLUTELY NO EXPECTATION OF RECEIVING ANYTHING IN RETURN FOR YOUR GIFT." (Emphasis mine)

A rather important point that was omitted, don't you think? You see, this statement makes Cash Gifting Illegal. When you receive your 'gift,' the gift made your gift subject to tax. The gift you received is taxable income. It is only non-taxable when it is a true gift, and the giver does not receive any compensation back in return for the gift. So now you have the IRS to deal with besides the possible civil and criminal charges you could be facing if law enforcement raids and shuts down the cash gifting program. Please don't just take my word on it. The FTC has this to say about Cash Gifting, and I quote:

"The Gifting Club "Gotcha" by the FTC:

When is a gift not a gift? When it's a "gotcha."

In a scam spreading throughout the mid-Atlantic states and the Pacific Northwest, people pay to join a "gifting club," billed in promotional materials as a private club with members eager to help new friends -- often from within their own neighborhood or church group.

In reality, the clubs are illegal pyramid schemes. New club members give cash "gifts" to the highest-ranking club members, with titles such as "captains." And they're promised that if they get additional members to join the club, they, too, will rise to become captains and receive money – far more than they initially paid to join the club -- from newer club "friends."

The problem is that, like most pyramid schemes, illegal gifting clubs must continually recruit ever-increasing numbers of members to survive. When the clubs don't attract enough new members, they collapse. Most members who paid to join the clubs never receive the financial "gifts" they expected, and lose everything they paid to join the club.

Don't Get on the Receiving End of a Gifting Club "Gotcha"

Promises of quick, easy money can be a powerful lure – especially when it comes with the additional benefit of new friendships.

If you're approached about joining a club but you aren't sure if it's an illegal gifting club, the Federal Trade Commission reminds you to:

- *Consider that a legitimate gift has no strings attached and is not an "investment."*
- *Avoid being misled into thinking a gifting club is legitimate because the ads say that members consider their payments a gift and expect nothing in return. This is an attempt to make an illegal transaction look legal.*

- *Be wary of success stories or testimonials of tremendous payoffs. Very few members of illegal gifting clubs or pyramid schemes ever receive any money.*
- *Take your time. Don't buckle under to a high-pressure sales pitch that requires you to join immediately or risk losing out on the opportunity. Remember, solid opportunities – and solid friendships – aren't formed through nerve-wracking tactics."*

To read more about this warning from the FTC, and how to file a complaint, visit their website:

http://www.ftc.gov/bcp/edu/pubs/consumer/alerts/alt056.shtm.

While the type of cash gifting is not the same as the format I have used, it does not change cash gifting is illegal, and it is an illegal pyramid.

Is this a pyramid?

Not at all. A pyramid is associated with an investment scheme, a company or a business. We are not a company, just a private sharing club. We have zero sales quotas, we do not sell positions. Everyone gives the same gifts, works together in a team and has the potential of receiving the same gifts.

Not true. The very nature of the program makes it an illegal pyramid scheme. Also the FTC stipulates Cash Gifting is an illegal pyramid scheme when they stated (in the quote I referenced above): "The problem is that, like most pyramid schemes, illegal gifting clubs must continually recruit ever-increasing numbers of members to survive."

If you still doubt this is not a pyramid, given the example I have provided, take a sheet of paper and map it out for yourself. If you give to 3 above you, and there are 3 below you, and each person has 3 above and below, you will readily see it forms a pyramid. Unless new people continue to join, it will all collapse."

How did this concept begin?

Giving private gifts to one another is an expression of kindness, which has been going on for centuries. Governments have allowed its practice for individuals to share their wealth with families, friends and others. It has been a means of helping and blessing others on special occasions or when the need arises. Many cultures gift as a matter of course. Asian, Jewish and South American communities gift individuals within their culture on a regular basis so that they may start a business or buy a home. They in turn gift someone else to help enhance their lives. Habitat for Humanity is a great example of private gifting. Everyone participates with their time, their talents and materials to build a home for someone else. Some participate with a hammer, some with nails, some with food and others with the monetary gifts to purchase the supplies, but all create a team that works together to bless someone's life.

Now all of this sounds really good, it is meant to, but means nothing. They are comparing apples to oranges. It is designed to make you feel good about being part of this illegal scheme. When a family member "gifted" to another family member for him or her to start a business, buy a house, pay for college, he or she weren't expecting to get thousands of dollars back in return for their 'gift."

Giving to Habitat for Humanity is a poor example because it is an official 501(c)3 Public Benefit Charitable Corporation. No-one you will be "gifting" to in this scheme is a 501(c)3 Public Benefit Charitable Corporation, and you are expecting to receive "gifts" in return. Habitat for Humanity does not give you any 'gift money' back for your 'cash gift' to them, but for your gift they give you a tax deduction.

How does Cash Gifting work?

This activity is offered only by means of an exclusive one-to-one invitation. When someone accepts the invitation, they can move through a natural progression from the giving to the receiving stages of the activity. In this activity, there is no fixed hierarchy of individuals who have an advantageous position or unfair advantage over new participants.

Again, this is meant to convince you this is legal. As previously shown, when you gift to someone, it must be given without any expectation of receiving anything in return. Here they clearly state you will move from the giving stage to the receiving stage, which means you are expecting something in return for your gift.

Who can participate?

This is a private sharing group, and is offered only through an exclusive one-on-one invitation to individuals over 18 years of age who live in the United States. You are invited to learn more about our activity and become part of something extraordinary.

Anyone can do this. Whether you are currently employed part-time or full-time, retired, unemployed, disabled, a student, single parent or a busy housewife; all you have to do is be willing to give!

Now did you really expect them to tell you that you had to meet some strict requirements or conditions before you could become part of this program? Of course not, for they would not have anyone joining if they did. Notice they only emphasized the giving, not the receiving as they did before.

Is this a company?

There isn't a company. We are a team of individuals and we give "Gifts" to one another. We are not a business or an investment. A company can't withhold or misplace our gift. We are totally in control and in charge of our own gifts and give directly one to another.

Again smoke and mirrors. There is a name for this entity, isn't there? You do have to join the organization before you can "gift" don't you? While it may not be an official "company" format, you are still joining an organization, and there are people running it.

Do I Need a Computer to Participate?

You will need to check your online back-office several times each week. For those who don't have a computer, consider having a family member, friend, or Inviter, with a computer, help you get started. Please be sure it is someone you know, love and trust! In most areas, public libraries have Internet ready computers available to the public and staff who will teach you the basics of how to use them.

Yes you do. They just don't want to come out and tell you so directly. They are afraid if they do, you won't join if you don't have one.

How can you give to a stranger?

How many times have you given to United Way, the Salvation Army and other charities? You don't know who got the gift, what stranger. The only difference here is that this person will start out as a stranger, but you will get to know them as part of the team, work with them and perhaps develop new friendships. We all have met some of the most wonderful people and have made a lot of new friends across the country and the world. These people are giving, they like team dynamics - they are people we want to meet and befriend.

This is really grasping at straws trying to convince you that giving to strangers is no different from giving to the United Way, Salvation Army, or some other charity. At least they are 501(c)3 Public Benefit Charitable organizations, unlike this entity consisting of a group of people whom you have no clue who they are: but are promising you riches through gifting.

Why would I want to participate?

"Gifting" has changed countless lives for the better. People who were about to lose their cars and homes have been saved from financial ruin, college education's have been made possible, and nearly forgotten dreams have come true, all from participation in "Gifting".

This is their attempt to tell you your life will suddenly be changed forever for becoming involved in cash gifting. What they don't tell you is that 85% of the people who participate in cash gifting lose all their money they "gifted," and receive nothing in return. They also don't tell you that the top people in the organization have at least 3,5, or as many as 10 different aliases commanding the top tiers of the pyramid cash gifting scheme. Yes, they are getting paid multiple times at your expense.

Is Cash Gifting Legal?

*This is probably the number one question that pops up when people start to see the lucrative potential with this kind of activity, and it's certainly the first thing that we wanted to know too... after all, we have no interest in getting into any type of legal hot water, and we're sure you don't either, so here's what we found out. In researching this activity, it's important to keep in mind that there's no book out there that tells you what is legal in our society, only what is not legal. In the United States we have the Preamble, the Constitution and the Bill of Rights to protect a private citizen's rights to earn, pay taxes and give away property and cash as long as it's done according to the laws and codes of this country. The U.S. gifting rules are found in the IRS Tax Code, Title 26, Sections 2501-2504 and 2511. "**Click here**" for this document. In 2009 in the United States of America, the law states that one or more individuals can give a cash gift to another individual of up to $13,000 each per calendar year without any tax liability to either the giver or receiver of the gift, because the tax on the gift has already been paid. We also found that most well organized Cash Gifting programs require each participant to use some form of a Gifting Statement and/or Non-Solicitation form, which when signed, become binding agreements between two private individuals. These forms are used, it's said, to ensure the longevity and legality of a gifting program. So giving a gift of cash to someone, be it a friend, family member or a stranger is legal according to IRS code.*

I already covered this at the beginning of this analysis, I won't repeat all of it. BUT one thing that needs to be pointed out is that everything they say here is true up to a point, they just don't tell you all of the IRS Tax Code they love to reference. They omitted telling you that for your gift to be legal, you must have ABSOLUTELY NO EXPECTATION OF RECEIVING ANYTHING IN RETURN FOR YOUR GIFT. This sentence alone makes their claim of legality false because cash gifting is all about "receiving" your gift for being in the program.

Now you have seen how they use omission to make you believe this is all legal, appeal to your sense of "giving," use smoke and mirrors by comparing unlike situations making you believe they are the same and equal; all to get you to join their illegal pyramid scheme. When they have you roped in the program, now they will teach you how to send your cash gift. I am not going to list all the instructions again they give you about how to send the money, what you have to do on your website to complete the notification of sending the gift, but I am going to list how they teach you to break the law. I have underlined key elements of what they are telling you to do, and also what they tell you to do that is illegal:

When sending anything by either USPS or private courier (e.g., FedEx, UPS, DHL, etc.), powerful scanners look into that envelope to make sure there is no contraband in the envelope and USPS and UPS have restrictions against sending cash. So, to prevent any problems with your sending cash gifts, follow these procedures to the letter.

If you do not follow these procedures, you will jeopardize the safety and longevity of the activity, so please be mindful of them:

1. <u>Take the cash and wrap it in black paper.</u>

2. <u>Write a brief note on a regular, 8 1/2 by 11, white sheet of paper,</u> such as: Hi Bill, Nice chatting with you! I am sending you this little gift of ($Amt.) to cheer your day and say thanks for your friendship. Have a nice day, (Your Name & Username). <u>Fold that paper in three and put the black paper inside it.</u>

3. <u>Take that folded white sheet of paper and fold a sheet of black construction paper</u> (purchased at any Art Supply Store or Office Supply Store, such as Staples, Office Depot, or Office Max) around it.

4. Put the folded sheet of black construction paper in a #10 SECURITY ENVELOPE, address the TO and FROM on the envelope, put a stamp on it, and put it in the mail.

5. When sending larger gifts by private courier (e.g., FedEx, UPS, DHL, etc.), do Steps 1 through 4, above, and put the smaller envelope in a manila folder (cut off the tab at the top part so it fits in a Priority Mail or private courier envelope) or old magazine (so it doesn't bounce around), and put it in the larger courier envelope.

6. <u>It is very important that your small envelope containing the cash is addressed (To and From), sealed, and stamped. This is in case the larger, courier envelope should be in an accident, damaged and opened, and your smaller envelope with the cash falling out</u>- you and your cash are protected because it is against the law to open an addressed, sealed, stamped envelope; it must be put in the mail right away and sent back on its way.

7. Your first few levels of gifts (Steps 1-3) can be sent via the Postal Service (USPS). DO NOT use a Delivery Confirmation Form! This will SLOW down your delivery and you need the gift to arrive as quickly as possible.

8. <u>Beginning with Step 4 gifts ($100), you MUST send these using a private courier (e.g., FedEx, UPS, DHL, etc.) using TRACKING NUMBERS. DO NOT indicate in any way that there is "cash" in the envelope, for your own safety and protection.</u> We recommend you send it Overnight Delivery. If it is okay with the person you are sending the gift, you can send it without having a "Signature Required." Some people are not home during the day to give a signature and do not mind having the envelope left at their door- it is entirely up to them, so please respect their wishes.

Congratulations, if you followed their instructions, you have broken the law just in sending the cash gift, let alone being a part of an illegal pyramid scheme. If this is so "Legal," why are they having you disguise your sending your cash gift, and having you breaking the law in doing so? Do you still think these cash gifting schemes are legal, no matter what format they use? Hopefully you now realize they are all illegal, and not to participate in them. Of course lately to encourage more Christians to participate, many of the new programs claim these programs are ordained by God, and they quote Scripture to prove they are legal. Well, God also says: "Do not steal." It was a commandment, not a suggestion. Now I could quote more Scripture to counter the Scripture they use taken out of context, but it is has nothing to do with these cash gifting schemes being illegal.

In the court case regarding the illegal cash gifting scheme "Women Empowering Women," which several of the leaders were sent to prison for their roles, the court makes a definitive ruling of the cash gifting scheme as being an illegal pyramid. Here is just one of the court cases:

IN THE SUPERIOR COURT OF THE U.S. VIRGIN ISLANDS DIVISION OF ST. THOMAS AND ST. JOHN;   SMALL CLAIMS No. 16/2006/ No. 17/2006 Action for Debt:

 JENNIFER CALLWOOD and DERRICK CALLWOOD, Plaintiffs; CASSANDRA VINCENT and MIGUEL PEREZ, Plaintiffs   vs ELIZABETH CRUSE, Defendant

I am only going to provide excerpts of the key points made by the judge in this proceeding. If you would like to read the entire ruling, you may read it here:

http://www.vid.uscourts.gov/territorial/06sc0016.pdf. From the ruling:

FACTUAL BACKGROUND: On or about September 19, 2005, *pro se* Plaintiffs, Mr. Derrick and Mrs. Jennifer Callwood and Ms. Cassandra Vincent and Mr. Miguel Perez (collectively "Plaintiffs") separately gave $5,000.00 to Defendant, Ms. Elizabeth Cruse ("Defendant") to join a group known as the "Women's Gifting Circle" ("Women's Gifting Circle" or "Circle"). Plaintiffs claim that in consideration of the $5000, they expected to receive $40,000.00 in two weeks. When they did not receive the money, Plaintiffs approached Defendant and requested the return of their $5000.00. Defendant refused. Plaintiffs brought these actions, claiming that Defendant was indebted to them for the $5,000.

At trial, Plaintiffs testified regarding their intentions and expectations in entering the Circle and proffered a nine (9) page document1 describing the "Circle." The document set forth, *inter alia*, the operation of the Circle and the duties of the various levels of its members and states in pertinent part:

Each woman who participates gives a gift of $5,000 to another woman in the circle. Each of us who have entered the circle have given that same gift to one of our sisters. Within the circle you enter, there are a total of 15 women at any given time who participates...Each woman "cycles" through the circle as new women join, ultimately receiving the sum of $40,000...2

Though Defendant denies that the Circle is a "pyramid scheme", the diagram of the "Table"

Resembles an inverted pyramid of fifteen (15) positions.3 The first level consists of eight (8) "appetizers". The next level consists of four (4) "soup and salad" positions, followed by two (2) entrees" leading up to the one (1) dessert."4 The object, more or less, is to move from "appetizer" to "dessert" to get the $40,000.00 by paying in the entry amount $5,000.00 and getting as many other women to join as possible.

The document also outlines the "rules" of the Circle which Plaintiffs would have to follow to "fulfill [their] obligation"5 and "receive support."6 Essentially, Plaintiffs were required to "gift" $5,000.00 by money order, cashier's check or cash7 to Defendant and sign a "Gifting Statement" declaring the money so given "is a gift, freely given to [Defendant] without consideration...This is strictly a gift and I expect nothing in return."

The Callwood Plaintiffs testified that they did not sign nor give Defendant the "Gifting Statement." Defendant, on the other hand, testified otherwise and proffered a "Gifting Statement," allegedly signed by Plaintiff Mrs. Jennifer Callwood. However, Mrs. Callwood testified that the handwriting on the Gifting Statement is not hers and that her name is misspelled. In the case of Plaintiffs, Vincent and Perez, both testified that neither of them signed a Gifting Statement. Nonetheless, in both cases, Defendant maintained that the funds were given to her as a gift and as such Plaintiffs have no right to their return.

Based upon the testimony of the parties and witnesses and the exhibits, *the Court found that there was no donative intent on the part of Plaintiffs to* give Defendant their money. Based upon this finding the Court concluded that as a Court sitting in Equity, the doctrine of "unjust enrichment" required that Defendant reimburse Plaintiffs the monies given to her by them. It therefore entered Judgment for Plaintiffs, whereupon Defendant immediately filed a "Notice of Appeal" and moved to stay the Judgments pending appeal.

The Quasi-Contractual Relationship Between the Parties. Defendant is also not likely to succeed on appeal given the nature of the relationship between the parties. The essence of the parties' relationship is one of quasi-contract. A claim of quasi-contract "is not a 'real' contract based on mutual consent and understanding of the parties."

To recover on a claim of quasi-contract, Plaintiffs must show (1) that they conferred a benefit upon Defendant; (2) that Defendant accepted the benefit; and (3) that the retention of the benefit by Defendant would be unjust and result in an inequity. Thus, "the essence of a quasi-contract claim is not the expectancy of the parties, but rather the unjust enrichment of one of them."

In the instant case, there can be no doubt that Plaintiffs conferred a benefit upon Defendant. Plaintiffs separately gave her $5,000.00 in the belief that they were entering into an agreement to have the money refunded to them eight-fold in two weeks time. It is uncontroverted that Defendant accepted the benefit and testified to receiving the funds. She further testified that she received it in relation to the Circle.

Allowing Defendant to retain the funds would result in an injustice for several reasons. Plaintiffs did not request that Defendant pay the $40,000.00 they expected to receive from participating in the Circle. Rather, they simply requested the money delivered to Defendant be returned to them as they no longer wished to participate in the Circle. In desiring to exercise their right to opt out of the circle, the testimony of the witnesses showed that others have opted out of the Circle and have had their monies or some portion thereof returned to them.

The Defense of Gifting. (KEY ELEMENTS):

At trial, Defendant maintained that the Plaintiffs simply bestowed a gift upon her. The gratuitous nature of such an act will negate a claim of unjust enrichment, as one cannot be unjustly enriched by something freely given. The essential elements which must be present to effectuate a gift are (1) donative intent; (2) delivery; and (3) acceptance. "There must be a clear, unmistakable, and unequivocal intention on the part of a donor to make a gift of his or her property in order to constitute a valid, effective gift...".

The testimony and evidence reveal insufficient proof of donative intent for three main reasons. First, Plaintiffs manifest intent and purpose in joining the Circle was never gratuitous in nature. Plaintiffs filed the Complaint stating that they "entered into an agreement that [they] would pay in $5000 and receive $40,000.00." Thus, Plaintiffs were operating from the standpoint of an agreement, not a gratuity. **Additionally, Plaintiffs testified they did not intend to merely provide a gift to Defendant. Their intent from the very beginning in furnishing the money was for one purpose and one purpose only, i.e., a short-term "investment". Their intent was to obtain a return on their "investment", not to make a gift to a person they did not even know. Thus, they never had the requisite donative intent at the time they provided Defendant with the money.**

Second, the relationship between the parties is akin to a business transaction and based on bargain and exchange. Plaintiffs testified that Police Officer Doss approached them and persuaded them to give her the money in order to receive $40,000.00. It was clear that if Plaintiffs gave up the $5,000.00 for a couple weeks, they would in return get their money back eight-fold. Not only were they expected to give the $5,000 but they also had to find another person to join the Circle. The fact that Plaintiffs had duties once they relinquished there monies **illustrates that they were conducting themselves as if**

they had an agreement (an important element). Even Defendant herself, in examining Plaintiff Miguel Perez, **stated that the relationship between herself and Plaintiffs was "considered an agreement." Thus, she understood that Plaintiffs were not intending to give a gift, but rather, intended to enter into an agreement whereby she would return their monies plus $35,000 in about two weeks.** Defendant knowingly induced Plaintiffs through the medium of Officer Doss to pay her based upon false promises of repayment. **She cannot now say that it was just a gift when she knew Plaintiffs' intentions were otherwise** (The "Gotcha Clause referenced by the FTC). Moreover, the ability to "opt out" of the Circle and have the "investment" monies refunded belies any donative intent on the part of Plaintiffs.

Moreover, **the ability to "opt out" of the Circle and have the "investment" monies refunded belies any donative intent on the part of Plaintiffs.** Plaintiffs testified that Defendant made numerous promises to them to return their $5000. Plaintiff Derrick Callwood testified that he called Defendant thirty-eight (38) times between October and November of 2005 and that Defendant assured him time and time again that he would get a full refund. Defendant denies promising Plaintiff that she was going to pay him back. In fact, at least one individual received a refund or some portion of the $5,000 deposited. Specifically, Officer Doss testified that two members of the circle, a Ms. Blackman and Ms. DeCastro were fully or partially refunded after they exercised their right to opt-out of the Circle. Plaintiff Cassandra Vincent also testified that Defendant gave her the option to get out of the Circle and have her money returned to her.

Third, the **"Receipt of Gift", identified in both cases as Plaintiff's Exhibit No. 1, does not substantiate Defendant's contention that the money given to her by Plainitffs was a gift.** Officer Doss testified that she delivered the monies on behalf of Plaintiffs Callwood to Defendant. Defendant then executed a "Receipt of Gift" and caused same to be delivered to Plaintiffs. **Simply referring to the funds as a gift does not make it so and does not negate Plaintiffs' non-donative intent.**

Additionally, the "Gifting Statement" cannot establish donative intent. Plaintiffs Vincent and Perez' uncontroverted testimony was that they never executed the Statement. With respect to Plaintiffs Callwood, as noted heretofore, Plaintiff Jennifer Callwood testified that her name on it was in effect a forgery.

The document itself is replete with the expectation of receiving monies in exchange for the $5,000.00. **Even though the word "gift" or some variation thereof is used over two dozen times, a rational reading of the document negates donative intent on the part of the persons involved.** By participating in the Circle and by providing funding and persuading other women to do the same, Plaintiffs expected to "ultimately receiv[e] the sum of $40,000." Pls. Ex. 2 at 1. Other phrases that contradict any donative intent include: "It is the intention of this community that at no time will anyone ever lose." Id. at 2. "Please know that by inviting you, we are asking you to receive support." Id. "we are accountable to each other and ourselves." These phrases taken together and read as a whole tend to illustrate a bargain and exchange relationship. The purpose is clear, i.e., "The Circle intends to "ultimately [pay] $40,000" in exchange for $5,000.00, if you perform your duties as outlined." **Plaintiffs had no intention of giving a "gift" but rather every intention and expectation of "investing" their money to make a high return.**

Most significant is the timing of Plaintiffs' receipt of the document, gift receipt and gifting statement—after they gave Defendant their money. At no time before relinquishing their money were Plaintiff informed that they would be "gifting it." Donative intent cannot be ascribed to them by Defendant after receiving the monies. **Donative intent must be manifested in the donors at the time they donate.** Here, the evidence clearly shows Plaintiffs never manifested any intent to donate funds to Defendant.

Equitable Relief. The Court entered Judgment in favor of Plaintiffs based upon the theory of unjust enrichment. "Unjust enrichment is an equitable remedy, typically invoked in quasi-contractual settings, where the plaintiff seeks to recover for a benefit he conferred unto the defendant under an unconsummated or void contract."

Here is what the Washington State Attorney General has posted on their website about cash gifting, and I quote:

Washington law declares the following practices illegal under the Anti-pyramid Promotional Schemes Act:

(1) No person may establish, promote, operate, or participate in any pyramid scheme.

(2) A limitation as to the number of persons who may participate, or the presence of additional conditions affecting eligibility for the opportunity to receive compensation under the scheme, does not change the identity of the scheme as a pyramid scheme.

(3) It is not a defense under chapter 65, Laws of 2006 that a person, on giving consideration, obtains goods, services, or intangible property in addition to the right to receive compensation, nor is it a defense to designate the consideration a gift, donation offering, or other word of similar meaning."

There is one point I do want to repeat to emphasize how people are fooled into being a part of these illegal schemes; and it is this one. The people who start these programs all use multiple aliases to trick people into thinking there are many people in this program, and to hide they are the primary ones who will be getting any gifting of any significant amount in the initial round. Many will allow the first round of gifting to be cycled (meaning everyone who initially joined receives their "gift." But it is in the second round when it all starts to unravel. Of course they have a built-in excuse. "The people who were to 'gift' failed to do so, therefore, it is the members fault for not being honest and 'gifting.' This is how this scheme is played. As I said before, 85%, and some cases even as high as 95% never receive their "promised gift." They merely take the money, then wait a while and re-open another gifting program under a new name for the program, and of course new names of the people running it, who are really the same people who stole your money the first time. Of course this time they will claim their program is not like all the other failed gifting programs, as they have solved the problems inherit in these programs. The same smoke and mirrors they used to get you to join the first time, is the same smoke and mirrors they use to get you to join their second program. Since you don't know they are one and the same, you fall prey once more to the hype of how this gifting program will change your life forever. Depending on how much they ask you to "gift" will make a difference in your life alright. It will just be your bank account is a lot lighter, while theirs got a lot fatter.

The sad part of this type of illegal pyramid scheme is the vast majority of the people who join these programs do not see the ruined: relationships, families, marriages, divorce, depression, and yes sad to say, even a few suicides from becoming involved in one of these gifting programs. This is the dark underbelly of cash gifting that no-one wants to talk about. Here is the story from someone who was in a cash gifting scheme, and what happened to this person. Reprinted here with permission, but the person wanted to remain anonymous:

The Reality of Cash Gifting, by Anonymous:

I got involved with a cash gifting opportunity a few years ago. I stumbled across it when I walked into a friend's house and overheard part of a conference call she was on. She tried to shut me out, but I was curious so I listened. It sounded really fun and very simple and quick way to make some easy money. I'd never heard of MLM or pyramid scams or anything like that. But I did know some of the people on that call and they were respectable citizens. Those I didn't know were all talking about their successes too. They all had good jobs, sounded educated…so I figured that they knew more then I obviously did and I always thought about investing my money somewhere— so that was my chance. (so to speak).

Not really understanding the process, but definitely willing to take the risk…I cash gifted $5000. Our particular opportunity was cash gifting WOMEN only. We had a sheet of rules (no one used last names—some used nicknames—first clue), we had a conf call each week, and we shared this opportunity with family and close friends.

I entered this opportunity in November and became really excited and shared the opportunity with all my close friends and family. My mother, my sister, my best friends....great! I watched as my name slowly shifted down the list and by April...I received all of my gifts, $40,000 CASH. I gifted myself back on another board and sat back as my friends jumped on and started moving through it. After all seeing was believing, and I made my money.

In August of that same year, I discovered what Pyramid Schemes actually were and how I was involved with one. This thing blew wide open in my community and surrounding communities. People got arrested and many struggled to find money to pay back what they could and try to keep everyone quiet. The Attorneys General website had a great article on the exact program I was involved with. I would spend time reading about it on the internet and watched the daily news as more people were getting caught and stepping forward. No charges were pressed IF you agreed to pay the money back. However, state lines had been crossed and this thing was traced to 5 states south and east of me!

To make a long story...longer...I hired a Criminal Defense Attorney. I wanted to protect myself from a lawsuit and prepare myself for the worst. Every day, I WATCHED out my window as the police car would make its rounds in the neighborhood. I watched as people I knew struggled with the stress of all of this, friends turned on each other, family members turned on each other...it was very destructive. I was not able to get my money back from the people I gifted as they were in another state. But I had to take out a loan against my home to pay back all that I had been given. I can joke about it now and honestly say that there is something harder than making $40K...it's paying it back after you thought it was yours!

My family and friends recovered from this. Some people created Gag orders and had people sign them and agreed to settle on ½ the amounts. Some insisted on full amounts...and a few agreed to let it go completely (realizing that they gave it as a gift). I know some people that got away with it and still worry about this coming back to them one day. I've heard tons of rumors about me...that I made hundreds of thousands in this scheme...ha! I have a nice 2nd mortgage that would tell a different story. But I keep quiet. I don't want the stress of what this brought into our lives to EVER happen again.

Experience comes in all shapes and sizes and this was a life lesson that I will never forget. I'm thankful that I got out from under it, but I would RUN from any type of GIFTING opportunity if it was presented to me. It's totally a scam. People lose. It's not possible to gain anything unless you are close to the top of the person who created it. And, just in case you're wondering, I traced my gifting scam back to the originator and she knows it. It wasn't that far back and I was amazed at how close to the beginning I really was....but there were SEVERAL boards going to get to me.

I don't care what someone calls this multi level gifting opportunity...it can be a business of ANY name. BUT...if it forms the shape of a triangle and your only way of success is by the introduction of new members....you may want to take a serious second look before getting involved. And if you are so bold as to say it's legal...that's fine too. I'm sure there are loopholes that continue to emerge....but remember...you MUST be close to the beginning to collect. After all....several people will fail for you to succeed....and in my book...that's not really success at all. That's greed.

Let's recap

Contrary to what they claim, the IRS Tax Code does not support cash gifting is legal;

Contrary to what they say, they are an illegal pyramid scheme,

They have to teach you how to break the law to send your gifts, all the while claiming they are legal entities,

No matter how they claim they have removed all the problems with cash gifting programs being illegal, thus making their program legal is a lie.

The FTC says Cash Gifting is Illegal

The 50-state attorneys general say Cash Gifting is Illegal

When you receive your 'gift,' it eliminates your 'gift' being tax-deductible, and any 'gift' you receive you must report it as income and be taxed on it. Failure to do so is tax-evasion.

At least 85% of the people joining a cash gifting program will never receive any gift, and in some programs it runs as high as 95%. Bottom line is you lose whatever amount you gifted.

Why your E-mail is not safe, and the Nigerian 419 E-mail scams next.

The Nigerian 419 E-mail Scams

We have all seen them in our E-mail Inbox, the Nigerian 419 E-mail scams. The irony of these scams is that they get their name from the Nigerian Penal Code (Section 419) making them illegal. While it is true that vast majority of us do not fall for these scams, the sad truth is there are enough people who do, and it causes them a financial disaster. You have to understand how many new people (called 'newbies' in the trade) for the first time enter the Internet every day worldwide. These are the targets of these scammers. They have no clue these E-mails are a scam, or how they work. They just see it as a means to get them out of a financial nightmare, and become a victim. If these E-mails truly were not effective, you would not still be getting them in your inbox.

The story line varies from E-mail scam to E-mail scam, but here are the typical ones going around today:

A widow is dying, and her late husband has left her a fortune. The reason for her illness varies, but the most common illness is she is suffering from some type of cancer. They had no children, so she wants to give you the money (usually in the millions of dollars) to carry on good charitable works with the money. Of course for you to get the money, you have to pay 'fees' before the money gets to you. But then what's a few hundred dollars when you will get millions? Of course something always happens that causes the fees to go up, and they need more money before they can send you the money. After they have done this three or four times, or you have run out of money first, they suddenly disappear. By this time you are out thousands of dollars, but of course will never receive the promised riches. Here are a couple of examples of this typical E-mail exactly as received using this format:

From: "Mrs Haley Anderson" <mrshalands@aol.com>
Sent: Tuesday, September 07, 2010 8:37 AM
To:
Subject: STOP CONTACTING THEM!!!

Atn: My Dear,

I am Mrs Haley Anderson, I am a US citizen, 48 years Old. I reside here in New Braunfels Texas. My residential address is as follows. 108 Crockett Court. Apt 303, New Braunfels Texas, United States, am thinking of relocating since I am now rich. I am one of those that took part in the Compensation in Nigeria many years ago and they refused to pay me, I had paid over US$28,000 while in the US, trying to get my payment all to no avail.

So I decided to travel down to Nigeria with all my compensation documents, And I was directed to meet Barrister Geoffrey Okafor, who is the member of COMPENSATION AWARD COMMITTEE, and I contacted him and he explained everything to me. He said whoever is contacting us through emails are fake. He took me to the paying bank for the claim of my Compensation payment.

Right now I am the most happiest woman on earth because I have received my compensation funds of $1,800,000.00. Moreover, Barrister Geoffrey Okafor, showed me the full information of those that are yet to receive their payments and I saw your name as one of the beneficiaries, and your email address, that is why I decided to email you to stop dealing with those people, they are not with your fund, they are only making money out of you. I will advise you to contact Barrister Geoffrey Okafor.

You have to contact him directly on this information below.

COMPENSATION AWARD HOUSE

Name : Barrister Geoffrey Okafor
Email: att_geoffreyokfor@mail.kz
TelPhone: +234 703 667 4681.

You really have to stop dealing with those people that are contacting you and telling you that your fund is with them, it is not in anyway with them, they are only taking advantage of you and they will dry you up until you have nothing and make sure you send him your full details.

The only money I paid after I met Barrister Geoffrey Okafor was just US$580.00 for the paper works, take note of that Once again stop contacting those people, I will advise you to contact Barrister Geoffrey Okafor so that he can help you to Deliver your fund instead of dealing with those liars that will be turning you around asking for different kind of money to complete your transaction.

Thank You and Be Blessed.

Mrs Haley Anderson.

Another One:

From: MADAM JOY WILLIAMS tropical@hol.gr

Date: Tuesday, January 12, 2010 6:37 AM

To: none

Subject: BELOVED IN FAITH,FROM MADAM JOY WILLIAM

FROM MADAM JOY WILLIAMS

PLOT 204,WILSON CLIFFORD CLOSE

VICTORIA ISLAND LAGOS,NIGERIA.

PRIVATE EMAIL; madamjoywiliams@hotmail.com

PLEASE ENDEAVOR TO USE THE FUND FOR THE LESS PRIVILEGED.

Dear,

I am the above named person . I am married to Dr. Kazeem williams, who worked with Kuwait embassy in Nigeria for nine years before he died in the year 2004. We were married for eleven years without a child. He died after a brief illness that lasted for only four days. Before his death we were both lived happily. Since his death I decided not to re-marry or get a child outside my matrimonial home, When my late husband was alive he deposited the sum of$12 Million (Twelve Million U.S. Dollars) with a Bank Oceanic (OCEANIC BANK PLC).

Presently, his money is still under the safe keeping of the Bank.Recently, my Doctor told me that I would not last for the next three months due to my cancer problems. Though what disturbs me most is my stroke. Having known my condition, I decided to donate this fund to an organization or better still a faithful fearing individual that will utilize this money the way I am going to instruct here in.I want a fellow that will use this fund on, orphanages and widows assisting the needy and to ensure that the less privilege is well taking care of. I took this decision because I don't have any child that will inherit this money and my husband relatives are not reliale enough to inherit this fund and I don't want my husband's hard earned money to be misused by unfaithful people.

I don't want a situation where this money will be used in an ungodly manner. Hence the reasons for taking this bold decision.

I am not afraid of death hence I know where I am going. I don't need any telephone communication in this regard because of my health and as well because of the presence of my husband's relatives around me always. I don't want them to know about this development.all my emails are confidentially wrote by my nurse aid in the hospital.

As soon as I receive your reply I will forward your personal informa-tion to my lawyer so that he will contact you as the legal owner of this fund before transferring the fund into your nominated Bank Account in your country. I will also issue you a letter of authority that will empower you as the original-beneficiary of this fund.

Please assure me that you will act accordingly as I stated here in.Once I hear from you I will give to you a lawyer that I have contacted to personal contact as to get intouch with him and know what is required of you, as to be able to do the needed things. Hoping to hear from you as soon as possible. Thanks.

My Very Best Regards,

Madam Joy williams

Please note all the typo's, misspelled words, and of course the improper grammar used in the E-mails. Notice the "To" line is blank or says none. Some say Undisclosed Recipients. Notice how they try to gain your trust and play on your sympathy. They know most people will over-look all the other dead-giveaways this is a scam, and contact them. Once you do, your E-mail is now sold to multiple scammers. You see, until you responded, they did not know if your E-mail address was real or not. That is why the 'To' line is blank, none or Undisclosed Recipients as they sent the E-mail 'bcc' and probably to at least 3-4 Million E-mail addresses.

Of course if this one doesn't get you, then they will try the "Your E-mail Has Won The Lottery" scam. Nothing has been changed in the E-mail, as was received as copied below. This one goes like this:

From: NOIKA PHONE PROMOTIONS nokia-lottery@nokia.com
To: Undisclosed Recipients
Subject: YOU HAVE BEEN SELECTED AMONG THE WINNERS

From The Desk Of The Promotion Officer

Nokia Mobile Phone Promotion
Alexander House,23-24
Courtfield Gardens,
London,SW5

England
Phone: +447-031-923-5661
Fax: +447-031-923-5661

WORLDWIDE ALLIANCE NOKIA PROMOTION.
Attention: Winner,

Due to global recession/economic melt down, The Nokia Company Worldwide organized Nokia Promotion to uplift the life of some well – meaning Individuals through the Nokia promotion as a mark of appreciation to the World. This is to inform you that you indeed one of the lucky winners of the ongoing Nokia promotion and your Email has been selected as one of the lucky winner of the Nokia promo.

Each winner is entitled of 900,000.00 GBP and you have been selected through our random Computer Ballot System.

We hereby advice you to forward the following information to enable us process your winning and payment from the Nokia Company's payment centers respectively.

1.Your full names:

2. Your complete address:

3. Your age:

4. Sex:

5. Occupation:

6. Marital Status:

7. Nationality:

8. Your Mobile Number:

Congratulations once again, please call after receiving this Email.+447-031-923-5661

Co-ordinator
MR. MR.STEVEN EVANS.

Phone:+447-031-923-5661
Fax: +447-031-923-5661

Or you can get back to us via email through Mrs.Doris Newman

(http://webmail.west.cox.net/do/mail/message/mailto?to=mrs.doris.
patricia.newman%40gmail.com)

CONGRATULATION   FROM   NOKIA   UNITED   KINGDOM
PROMOTION UNIT.

THANKS FOR BEING PART OF THIS PROMO.

Yours faithfully,
MANAGEMENT.
MR.STEVEN EVANS .
UK NOKIA PROMOTER.

Copyright ©2009 Nokia. All rights reserved.
....
....

This email and its attachments are confidential and intended for the
exclusive use of the addressee(s). This email and its attachments may
also be privileged or protected by legal rules. If you have received this
by mistake please let us know by reply immediately and destroy the
email and its attachments without reading, copying or forwarding the
contents.

What is interesting about this E-mail is that they used a Copyright and
confidentiality statement at the bottom of the E-mail to try to convince you
this is a legitimate E-mail. Simply put, if you did not purchase a lottery
ticket, you cannot win. If your E-mail was indeed used for you to win this
prize, then why didn't they use it in the "To" line? What does your age, sex,
marital status, nationality, and cell phone number have to do with your

winning the lottery? The answer is absolutely nothing. This is just a means to gather more information to steal your identity.

The latest trend in these Nigerian 419 E-mail scams is a military person who is stationed in Iraq has found a cache of cash, and needs your help to get it out of the country. This scam goes like this:

From: Sgt Dave Godwin
To: none
Subject: FROM SGT DAVE GODWIN(MESSAGE FROM IRAQ)
From Sgt Dave Godwin.

Good Day,

I found your contact particulars in an E-mail address guide that was provided to us here, as I desperately needed an urgent help to do this deal. I am seeking your kind assistance to move the sum of $15m {Fifteen Million U.S Dollars only} to you; as far as I can be assured that my share will be safe in your care until I complete my service here.

SOURCE OF FUND:

A lot of money in various currencies were discovered in barrels at a farmhouse near one of Saddam's old palaces in Tikrit in Iraq during an operation Conquest in Fallujah north of Baghdad, and it was agreed by Staff Sgt. Kenneth Buff and I that some part of this money be shared among both of us before informing anybody about it since both of us saw the money first. This is quite an illegal thing to do, but well tell you what? no compensation can make up for the risk we have taken with our lives in this hell hole, of which my brother in-law was killed by a road side bomb last time.

The above figure was given to me as my share, and to conceal this kind of money became a problem for me, so with the help of a British Contact working here, at Southern Basra British fortified green zone, whose office enjoys some immunity, I was able to get the package out to a safe location entirely out of trouble spot. He does not know the real contents of the package, and believes that it belongs to a British/American medical doctor who died in a raid here in Baghdad, and before giving up, trusted me to hand over the package to his family in United States. I have now found a much secured way of getting the package out of Iraq to you, for you to pick it up, and I will discuss this with you when I am sure that you are willing to assist me, and I believe that my money will be well secured in your hand because you have fear of God.

I want you to tell me how much you will take from this money for the assistance you will give me. One passionate appeal I will make to you is not to discuss this matter with anybody, should you have reasons to reject this offer, please and please destroy this message as any leakage of this information will be too bad and catastrophe for soldiers here in Iraq. I do not know how long we will remain here, but I hope to have a shift very soon for me to return back to the States. I have been shot and wounded twice and I have survived two terrible suicides bomb attacks just by special grace of God, this and other reasons I will mention later has prompted me to reach out for help, I will honestly want this matter be resolved immediately because the government of 'Mr President' is working hard to pull out of Iraq and if this happen which would be soonest,I may find it difficult to move the fund and this is more/other reason for my urgent call for assistance.

I thank you so much for everything and anticipate that you will be trustworthy and handle this transaction to the best of your ability to benefit both of us.

God Bless you and your family.
Yours
Sgt. Dave Godwin

As with the previous E-mails, this one is rife with typos, poor grammar, and of course they admit what they are doing, and asking you to do is illegal. But they hope your greed will overcome this minor stumbling block and you will contact him to help. Of course the reply will be the 'cost' to get this money out of Iraq to you, which you must pay. After all, you will receive millions, so this is just a minor cost compared to the total amount you will receive.

And magically, just like in the two previous types of scams, there are always surprise additional fees that have to be paid each time until they either bleed you dry or you stop sending them money. Rather odd he wants you, not a member of his family, to aid him isn't it.

The last example I am going to provide is an E-mail that is supposed to be coming from the FBI. It goes like this:

From: Ditullio_Nicholas ditul1oo@canton.edu
To: Undisclosed Recipients
Subject: FEDERAL BUREAU OF INVESTIGATION (FINAL NOTICE)

ROBERT MUELLER III
EXECUTIVE DIRECTOR FBI
FEDERAL BUREAU OF INVESTIGATION
FBI.WASHINGTON D.C

INTERNET

ATTENTION: BENEFICIARY,

The Federal Bureau of Investigation received a report of scam against you and other British/US citizens and Maylaysia, Etc.

The countries of Nigeria, Benin Republic, Burkinafaso And Ghana have recompensed you following the meeting held with the Four countries' Government and various countries' high commission for the fraudulent activities carried out by the Four countries' Citizens. Your name was among those scammed as listed by the Nigeria Financial Intelligent Unit (NFIU). Your compensation funds have been finally approved for transfer to you.

But We were made to understand that a lady with name Mrs. Joan C.Bailey from OHIO has already contacted them and also presented to them all the necessary documentations evidencing your claim purported to have been signed personally by you prior to the release of your compensation fund valued at about US$3,000,000 ,Please contact the Central Bank of Nigeria through the contact email given below and ask them to attend to your payment file asap. Please state your

FULL NAMES,
CITY,STATE,ZIP,COUNTRY,
SEX,
AGE,
TELEPHONE NUMBER
EMAIL ADDRESS.
NAME: Sanusi Lamido Sanusi
OFFICE ADDRESS: Central Bank of Nigeria,
Central Business District,
Cadastral Zone, Abuja, Federal Capital Territory, Nigeria.
Email: sanusilamidos066@yahoo.com.hk
Tel: +234-806-0935-542

Ensure you follow all their procedure as may be required by them as that will further help hasten up the whole procedure as regard to the transfer of your fund to you as designated. Also have in mind that the Central Bank of Nigeria equally have their own protocol of operation as stipulated on their banking terms, so delay could be very danger-ous. Thank you very much for your anticipated co-operation in ad-vance as we earnestly await your urgent response to this matter.

Best Regards,
Robert S. Mueller III
Federal Bureau of Investigation
J. Edgar Hoover Building
935 Pennsylvania Avenue, NW
Washington, D.C.
Private email : romueller100@sify.com

As you hopefully have learned by now, the first dead give-away is the "Undisclosed Recipients" in the "To" line. Also the Director of the FBI does not use a sify.com E-mail address, as shown in the signature line of the E-mail. I don't think they used "FBI" enough in the E-mail. I am sure you picked up on all the other glaring points in this E-mail that told you this was a scam.

Rather than give an illustration of all the different types of E-mails scams, and the deviations on all of them, here is a short list of the E-mail scams being received today:

DHL Courier for Loan Package	Scammed Victim
FBI-Report of a Scam Against You	Clinical Diplomatic Receipt Payment Letter
Next of Kin/Beneficiary	Bank Account on Hold
Business Proposal	Fund Transfer
Unpaid Beneficiary	International Certified Bank Draft/Cheque
Scammed Victim Compensation Fund	Need Your Urgent Assistance
UN & World Bank Payment	UN Scammed or Extorted Money Resolution
Your Intercepted Funds	ATM Cash Grant
Employment Offer	Stand-in Next of Kin
Western Union Money Transfer	Payment for Past Efforts
Agent Needed	Need Trustworthy Person
Compensation Claim	Security and Exchange Commission
Quick Investment Assistance	Senate Committee Approval Payment

I have not listed all the different types of E-mail scams that are flooding your inbox daily because there are over thirty different variations of each type of the E-mail scams I referenced above. It would take 25 pages to list them all, and then they would be outdated as new ones keep coming every month. But there are E-mails right now that can fool you, and these are the bank phishing scams, two E-mails that if you participate in them could land you in prison, and the latest job scam that will steal your identity and possibly clean out your bank accounts while running up your credit card debt. But before I discuss the Bank Phishing E-mail scams, here is a true story I wanted to share with you that still has me laughing:

In one of my throw-away E-mail accounts I received a Nigerian 419 E-mail scam. They claimed to be a legal firm that wanted me to stand in as the next of kin for a lady who was killed in the London Bus Bombings. They had tried unsuccessfully to find any surviving next of kin, thus why they wanted to use me so they could keep the bank from receiving $23 million dollars. For my services, I was to receive payment of 20% of the proceeds, and of course they get 80%. They even included links to newspaper articles where this lady's name was listed among the dead to convince me this was real.

So I responded to them and told them that while I appreciated their most generous offer, I could not in clear conscious accept their offer while there were relatives alive and well in London who were the rightful heir. I immediately got a return reply wanting to know how I could find the heir, when they had failed. They assured me no such heir existed. To which I responded, well in the newspaper links you provided me, they had a picture of her husband and child, and in the interview with him his address. I informed them I knew they would want him to contact them, so I had contacted him with their information so he could claim his rightful inheritance of the bank proceeds; as well as the law enforcement authorities in case they were needed for confirmation he was the deceased's husband and heir. Needless to say, I never heard from them again.

Now, let's talk about Bank Phishing E-mail Scams, and how easy it is for you to fall for one of them.

Bank Phishing E-mail Scams

Of all the types of E-mail scams going around today, the bank phishing E-mail scams are those who have become the most sophisticated of them all. In fact, they are so good, the FBI Director, Robert Mueller, almost became a victim of this scam. Speaking at the Commonwealth Club of California in San Francisco on cybersecurity he told this story:

He received an e-mail purporting to be from his bank that looked "perfectly legitimate" and which prompted him to verify some information. He started to follow the instructions but then realized that "might not be such a good idea," he said. "Just a few clicks away from falling into a classic Internet phishing scam," Mueller "barely caught himself in time" and admitted he "definitely should have known better."

He said he changed his passwords and tried to pass the incident off to his wife as a "teachable moment," but she was having none of it and told him, "It is our money. No more Internet banking for you!"

Now, if it could happen to him, it can happen to you. They are that good. So what makes these E-mails so easy to fall for? First, they 'scare' you into thinking something bad has happened to your bank account. The E-mail is reportedly from the bank's security head telling you there has been 'unusual activity' on your account, there has been a 'possible breach of security' on your account, or there may have been 'unauthorized people' attempting to access your account; and of course they need your 'immediate' attention to this matter. They want you to take immediate action, so they provide you a link to the bank's website for you to resolve this issue. The only problem is that the link does not take you to your online bank account, but to a clone site identical to your online banking website. Before you can exit this phony site, they have already accessed your real online bank account, and cleaned out your checking and savings accounts, and obtained your credit card information if it is also linked to your online banking. By the time you figure out you have been had, you go to your online banking and discover your accounts have been totally cleaned out. Later you discover that your credit card has been charged to the max as well.

To illustrate just how convincing these E-mails can appear, here is one I received supposedly from Bank of America. The Bank of America Logo has been removed by me, but the E-mail is as received:

From: Bank of America

To: None

Subject: Bank of America Alert Message Center

Confirm Your Account Information

Remember: Always look for your SiteKey before you enter your passcode during Sign In »

Dear Valued Bank of America Customer

IMPORTANT: Your online account information must be confirmed and verified to ensure uninterrupted service.

To enhance the level of service you receive with Bank of America Online Services, we regularly review the online banking accounts.

We have issued this warning message to inform you that we have detected a slight error in your account information. This might be due to either of the following reasons:

- A recent change in your personal information (i.e.change of address).
- Submiting invalid information during the initial sign up process.
- An inability to accurately verify your selected option of payment due to an internal error within our processors.

As a result, we require you to confirm and verify your account information By Clicking Here and completing the confirmation process.

Note

However, failure to confirm and verify your account information will result in temporarily account suspension. Please understand that this is a security measure intended to help protect you and your account. We apologize for any inconvenience. If you have any question regarding this, please call us at 888-692-5949, 24 hours a day, seven days a week. or simply Sign In to Online Banking and click on "Help".

Thank you for banking at Bank of America. We look forward to serving your financial needs for many years to come.

Because email is not a secure form of communication, please do not reply to this email.

If you have any questions about your account or need assistance, please call the phone number on your statement or go to Contact Us at www.bankofamerica.com.

Now here are the things I want to call to your attention that fools most people into believing this came from Bank of America if you are one of their customers:

Notice the statement at the top of the E-mail that tells you to look for your SiteKey before signing into your account. This is one of the security measures Bank of America uses when accessing your online banking. So this notice is intended to make you believe this is a real E-mail from Bank of America.

The "To" line says None. They know your E-mail address, but it is not used. A major Red Flag Warning.

They do not use your name in the body of the E-mail, but instead say 'valued customer." They know your name, another major Red Flag Warning.

The two links in the body of the E-mail when clicked will take you to a website that will appear to be Bank of America. Instead if you put your cursor over the link, you will see it will take you to:

www.thecordwainer.com/bofa.online/system/sercuredpage/. If this was from Bank of America, it would have shown: www.bankofamerica.com. On a PC this information will appear on the lower left hand side of your task bar when the cursor is over the URL. On a MAC, the image will pop up on your screen.

One last thing I want to point out about this E-mail and that is where at the bottom of the E-mail they say this:

Because email is not a secure form of communication, please do not reply to this email. If you have any questions about your account or need assistance, please call the phone number on your statement or go to Contact Us at www.bankofamerica.com.

This is true. This is just another way they want to fool you into believing this E-mail really is from Bank of America by stating please call the phone number on your statement or using the real Bank of America URL to login to your account.

When you see it with the Bank of America logo at the top and bottom of the E-mail, it makes the E-mail look even more convincing it is real. That is why we say they are very good at what they do, and they are getting even better. Still there are Red Flag Warnings that give these away, and one they cannot get around. They will never use your real E-mail address, but always the "To" line will be either blank, say none, or undisclosed recipients. They have to use the BCC so they can send this out to 2-4 million E-mail accounts. They do not have time to address each E-mail address. They are counting on you not noticing, and when you receive this panic at thinking you must take immediate action and not think it might be a fraudulent E-mail.

Just as with the Nigerian 419 E-mail scams, the reason they keep sending them is that people fall for them. If the FBI Director was almost fooled, anyone can be fooled into falling for them. Hopefully now you won't be one of them.

Not only are they sending out bank phishing E-mails, they are also doing the same thing for your credit cards. Whether it is American Express, Discover, Visa, MasterCard, Gas Cards, Store Cards, or any other type of credit card;

you are at risk of becoming a victim. Remember what Robert Mueller said: *"The phony bank E-mail looked perfectly legitimate."* That's what the conmen are counting on to trick you.

One more thing about your falling for one of these fake bank E-mails. When you do login to the fake website and they have captured your information for them to access your real online bank account, sometimes they will change your password so you cannot access your own online account. This prevents you from beating them to your account information to change your pin and set your new password. Now you have to call the bank to get them reset so you can access your account. Do not keep your account that was hacked. Open an entirely new bank account and savings account, and get a new credit card. For security purposes, I recommend for your online banking you have one online account for checking, one online account for savings and yet another online account for your credit card. Each account has its own unique pin number and password. I also recommend that you have security software that will scan your computer to make sure they did not place any spyware on your computer that allows them to access your online bank accounts. There are many fine software programs that will protect your computer from malware and spyware. Run regular scans of your system, not just on the routine maintenance scans your system makes. It is better to be safe than sorry. You don't want to get scammed twice.

LET'S RECAP:

Your E-mail cannot win you the lottery. The only way you can win a lottery is to purchase a ticket. If you do win the lottery, you do not have to pay anyone to get your winnings.

No dying widow picked you out of billions of people on this earth to have you distribute her wealth, and make you pay the fees for doing so. Especially when she doesn't know your name or your E-mail address.

No military person will share with you any money found in Iraq from Saddam Hussein's stashed fortune especially when they don't know you. Don't you think they would share it with a family member before sharing it with a totally anonymous person on the web first?

Bank phishing E-mails are getting better and better all the time at fooling you into falling for their pitch. Follow the guidelines presented so you know it is fake. Your bank will never ask you to click on a link in an E-mail to rectify any possible security breach or unusual activity in your bank account. They will direct you to their customer service center by telling you to login to your online banking, or have you call the 800 number on your card to resolve any issue.

While these Bank Phishing E-mail Scams are not only easy to fall for, but can be disastrous to your financial health, these next type of E-mail scams could possibly land you in prison if you become a victim. Here's how they work.

Two E-mails That Could Land You In Prison

There are two E-mails that if you become a victim of that could land you in prison. They are what is known in the trades as the Advance Fee/Money Mule E-mail Fraud and The Drop-Ship Mule E-mail Fraud. Before I go into how if you become a victim of these two types of E-mail Fraud could land you in prison, here is how they work:

The Advance Fee/Money Mule Scam

Let's set the stage for this E-mail Fraud and why you would be susceptible to fall for it: You are out of work, or you need to make additional money and want to work from home part-time. Then in your Inbox comes what you believe is the answer to your dreams: The chance to work from home part-time and make full-time money. Not only can you work from home and make good money, but also this is a job that is very easy for you to do. There are two versions of this scam. Here is the E-mail that you receive:

To: Undisclosed Recipient
From: STA Investments
RE: Account Receivable Officer

Dear Sir/Madam:

I represent STA Investments. STA Investments is one of the UK's premier real estate investment, ownership, development, operations, management, and leasing organizations. It owns a geographically diversified portfolio of residential communities.

Privately owned and operated from its headquarters in England and has branches in many other countries. The company took its real estate expertise, experience, tenacity, financial strength, keen foresight and commitment to new heights laying a sound foundation for significant growth.

Self-managed and steadfast in achieving excellence in all aspects of the commercial and residential real estate industry, STA Investments continues to raise the bar on tenant satisfaction, innovative and flexible leasing programs, property-management efficiency, geographical focus, and redevelopment strategies in order to achieve record revenue growth and profit returns.

STA Investments has grown steadily through the years. Rather than developing new properties, STA Investments typically purchases existing properties that have the potential to appreciate immediately with the application of improved management and marketing procedures.

We currently have two positions to fill on our team. Please visit our website to review the positions and qualifications for our openings:

http://www.STAInvestments.com.

Sincerely,

The STA Investment Team

Sounds great, so you go to their very impressive website, which gives you a lot of information about the company that is designed to impress you, and convince you this is a company that you want to work for. They then have you click on the position available tab and you see this explanation of the job of your dreams:

Account Receivable Officer

Thank you for being interested in the offer. Here are the details about the job. Please carefully read through.

We serve the entire United States and a growing export market, particularly in the monitoring of selected investment in different sector of the company. Superior products including Private Equity, Real Estate Investing, Corporate equity and others.

Your primary task, as a representative of the company is to coordinate payments from customers and help us with the payments processing. Once we have completed an investment monitoring process on our company behalf, our client will pay our company an Agreed sum of money as percentage.

About 90% of our customers from the United States prefer to pay through Check drawn from the United States Bank and it takes us longer time to handle such payment and the percentage charged as tax on International Money Transfer from Company is high compare to Individual. Because of the increasing number of clients, we have decided to open this new contract-to-hire job position for solving this problem.

Your Primary task (Collection of Payments):

1. Receive payment from our Customers or Clients.

2. Cash Payment at your Bank.

3. Deduct 10%, which will be your percentage/pay on Payment processed.

4. Forward balance after deduction of percentage/pay to any of the offices you will be contacted to send payment to.

You'll have a lot of free time doing another job because this job is part-time. Your Income or pay would be a minimum of $1,000 weekly depending on your level of competency and efficiency and how fast you can process the payments.

Get back to us with the below information so that we can add your mailing address to our regional database and the only reason why we need the following information is to enable our client addressed payment to you once we must have conducted the necessary background check.

After reading this, you know this is a job you can do; but more important you want to do. They provide you an online application form for you to fill out, which you do, and then you wait for their decision if you got the job. This is one form of this scam:

A few days later the good news arrives in your Inbox saying you are hired for this position. They attach information about what you need to do to fulfill this role, and you are good-to-go. Soon the checks come flooding in, which you process as instructed, and then wire the balance of the money to the recipient as instructed via Western Union. All is well with the world, and you are making $10-$40,000 dollars for your efforts. You have deposited the checks into your bank account that you have set up for these transactions, and you have wired the money to the party you were instructed. They use Western Union because the money cannot be traced once picked up.

Then the bottom falls out of your dream job. First after about 10 days they fire you, as they claim you did not follow their instructions correctly. If that is not bad enough, then the really big bombshell drops: All those checks you deposited came back as NSF. The reason they fired you in the 10 day period is that all the checks will be coming back within twelve to fourteen banking days. They don't want the checks coming back while you are still employed or you will know you were scammed. Now you must make good on the total dollar amount of all those checks. Because you wired at least 90% of the money, the majority of the time you will not have the money to make good 100% on these NSF checks. The bank tells you either you make good, or they will notify the authorities and have you charged with bank fraud, wire fraud, and possibly money laundering.

The other version of this scam is that the checks do clear, but after a couple of weeks you are fired. Then you learn from law enforcement that you have been part of a money laundering ring, and you now face charges of wire fraud, bank fraud, possibly money laundering, and a few more charges that will be listed below.

You see the only person in this whole scenario that is real is "You." The company that hired you is a fake company, the name of the person who hired you is a fake name, and the company and person to whom you wired the money Western Union also does not exist and is fake. The only person that law enforcement knows who is real and can find is "you."

So, what were the Red Flag Warnings that you should have noticed that would have prevented you from falling for this scam and becoming a victim?

First, the E-mail address line says: Undisclosed Recipients. They never use your name in the salutation. The body of the E-mail has grammar errors that a company of their claimed stature would not have. None of the information contained in the E-mail really says anything of value, but is only meant to impress you.

Second, when you go to the website, the Home Page is designed to further impress you, but here too there are many grammar mistakes that should be a warning. All the information provided about the company means nothing, but just words to impress you. In the example they listed two US addresses and phone numbers. The address in one case did not exist, and in the other it was a residential address. The phone numbers provided were invalid and not even a listing for the address and state provided. Even in the description of the position being offered there are grammar mistakes. All of these would not be present with a company that claims to be as reputable as they do. Their claim that it costs more for them to process checks from the U.S. is a lie. All reputable firms have payment made via bank wire, or electronic funds transfers.

What they didn't tell you is that for you to act as their money transfer agent: You must be a licensed money transfer agent, and you must be insured and bonded to act as a money transfer agent. Add these to the list of charges above, and you are in serious legal trouble.

THE DROP-SHIP MULE SCAM

This is very similar to the above Advance Fee/Money Mule Scam, but with a twist. Instead of sending you checks to process for the company, instead you will receive goods that you are to inspect for damage, and then forward the goods to the receiving company. They will provide you a credit card to cover your expenses, and you will receive a percentage of the value of the products or a flat fee as your fee for performing this job. Here is an example of the job description for this job:

REQUIREMENTS

- 1-2 years exp. with Shipping and Receiving
- Have the ability to lift 25lbs
- Must have a working and proficient knowledge of UPS, UPS Worldship, US Post Office, Fedex and other major carrier processes
- Interact with Freight Carriers
- Basic Knowledge of Microsoft Office (Packing List & Commercial Invoices)
- Positive Attitude
- Organizational Detail Oriented Skills
- Detail oriented with math skills
- Written and Verbal Communication Skills
- Interact with Quality Control (QC) to Verify Customer and Company Specifications are Met
- Stable internet connection at home
- Prepare and process shipping documents: Slips, Bills of lading, etc.
- Ensure product quality prior to shipping
- Coordinate deliveries and pick ups with carriers for before/after Hour shipments
- Follow directions and routines
- And Other Duties as Assigned

Base Pay: Starting salary is $70-80 per sent package

Employee Type: Full Time, Temporary/Contract/Project

Industry: Transportation/Warehouse

Manages Others: no

Job Type: Distribution - Shipping Transportation Warehouse

Req'd Education: Not Specified

Req'd Experience: 1-2 years

Req'd Travel: No

Relocation Covered: No

Candidates responding to this posting must currently possess the eligibility to work in the United States.

You are instructed to send your reports and expenses to the company usually in two-week increments. Then in two weeks you are to receive your payment for your services. But before you receive your payment, they fire you. Then you learn that you have been receiving stolen goods, using a stolen credit card, and again none of the parties in all of these transactions are real except you. Now you are facing charges of receiving and sending stolen goods, using stolen credit cards, fraud; and yes you must be licensed and bonded to perform these duties.

So what are the Red Flag Warnings for this E-mail scam?

Usually you are contacted by E-mail saying they saw your resume on *Monster* or *Craigslist* yet they use "Unregistered Recipients" as your E-mail address, and they do not reference you by name in the body of the E-mail. Now if they saw your resume on either of these two job sites, they would know your E-mail address and your name. Major Red Flag Warnings in this scam.

In the listing of the job requirements, they never mention your requiring to be insured and bonded to perform these duties. They also have typos and grammar errors in the content of the job description. Since they promoted this as a work-from–home opportunity, of course there would be no travel and relocation expenses. All they did was copy and paste a legitimate job description from another company to pass it off as their own.

Remember when I said falling for these E-mail Frauds could land you in prison? Well, even though you are a victim, the FBI is taking a totally different approach to people who participate in these scams.

Here is what The FBI's top anti-cyber crime official, Patrick Carney, acting chief of the FBI's cyber criminal section said:

"The agency is planning a law enforcement action against so-called "money mules," <u>individuals willingly or unwittingly roped into helping</u> organized computer crooks launder money stolen through online banking fraud or from drug money.

Mules are an integral component of an international crime wave that is costing U.S. banks and companies hundreds of millions of dollars. He said the agency hopes the enforcement action will help spread awareness that money mules are helping to perpetrate crimes.

"We want to make sure that public understands this is illegal activity and one of the best ways we can think of to give that message is to have some prosecutions," Carney said at a Federal Deposit Insurance Corporation (FDIC) symposium in Arlington, Va. today on combating commercial payments fraud. "We realize it's not going to make the problem go away, but it should help raise awareness and send a signal."

The mule recruitment process can be very convincing: Some scammers go through the trouble of conducting phone interviews, following those up with a barrage of online questionnaires. At some point in the recruitment process, however, the fictitious company will require the recruit to hand over their bank account numbers, so that the erstwhile employer can deposit their clients' funds. The employees eventually receive checks, wire transfers or automated clearing house (ACH) payments, and are asked to pull the money out of their bank in cash and wire the money overseas through establishments like Western Union and Moneygram. The typical "commission" for each transfer (most money mules get a single transfer before they're fired) is about 8 percent, minus the fees for wiring the money.

I have interviewed more than 150 money mules in the course of my investigations over the last year into this type of fraud. I can safely say that most mules fit into one of two camps: Those that are simply not the sharpest crayons in the box and really did get bamboozled (at least up to a point); and those who are out of a job, laid off, or otherwise in need of money and simply aren't asking themselves or anyone else too many questions about the whole process.

I find most mules fit into the latter group, and you can usually tell because these individuals often will admit to having set up a new account for the job – separate from where they keep their meager savings or checking. When pressed as to why they did this, if they're honest most will say they weren't sure about the whole arrangement and wanted to protect their investments just in case their employers turned out to be less-than-honest."

So even if you are a true victim, you cannot count on not going to prison if you fall for one of these E-mail Advance Fee-Money/Drop-Ship Mule scams. The reason simply is because these crimes are destroying local, state and national economies, and law enforcement has to send a message that if you play, you pay. Don't become a victim and pay the ultimate price that will follow you the rest of your life.

Adding insult to injury of these two scams is you have also opened yourself up to Identity Theft as these crooks have all your personal information that you gave them when you applied for these jobs.

But the scammers are not done with these fake job offers. Here is the latest job offer that is going around, and again they are getting the information from your resume posted on Monster or Craigslist, and it goes like this:

FAKE JOB OFFER

You have posted your resume on Monster and Craigslist looking for a job. One day in your Inbox you receive this E-mail (I have changed the actual recipient E-mail address, but everything else is as it was received):

Subject: Re: Outstanding Data Entry/Filing Clerk – Ima Fake
From: myofficestaffing@earthlink.net
To: imafake@hotmail.com
Date: Wed, 31 Mar 2010 15:01:51 -0700

Dear Ms.,

We've taken some time to look through the applications. And we've decided we'd love to have you as a part of our team! We'd like you to come in sometime before the end of the week for a face-to-face interview. This is for the Data Entry/Filing Clerk position, with compensation starting at $35,550 a year plus a benefit package which includes health, medical, dental and 401k after 30 days of employment.

We are REQUIRED to run credit and background checks on all our employees, due to the nature of the work and also due to sensitive documents and materials that will be easily accessible to you.

The credit check can be done now via this link:

http://bit.ly/aEbnNW It's free, no worries. We are also not judging your score, like I previously said, this is just a security requirement. After you have taken the credit check, send us the confirmation code via e-mail, and we'll set up an interview right away. We do not want to see any sensitive or private info via e-mail and the background check will be taken at our face-to-face interview.

For any questions, feel free to e-mail me. I am looking forward to speaking with you in person!

Sarah Murphy

After reading this, you are interested in obtaining an interview so you click on the link they provide to get your credit check. You fill in all the information, and you are excited about being contacted for your personal interview. All sounds good, right? Well all is not as it seems.

So what Red Flag Warnings have you spotted in the E-mail that told you this was a scam? Well, here are the Red Flag Warnings you should have caught:

The E-mail was sent to your E-mail that you provided in your resume, but they did not address you by name in the body of the E-mail. This information was available to them from your resume.

They have offered you the job before they do a personal interview, and they offered you the job via E-mail after only reviewing your resume. The personal interview is just a formality according to their E-mail. You also don't know if there is shift work involved and what shift you would be assigned; yet they have offered you the job.

The Major Red Flag Warning is the URL link they provided you for creditreport.com. While the site you are taken to looks exactly like creditreport.com using this URL link, it is a fake site. The real URL is www.creditreport.com. They used http://bit.ly/aEbnNW.com.

Another Red Flag Warning is the person from whom this E-mail was sent does not identify her title, telephone number, or personal E-mail address. Any HR person would have all this information in their signature line. Plus you have no idea of where this company is located as they do not provide an address or phone number. This E-mail is designed to steal your Identity, and also to make money from selling your E-mail address to other scam artists. Next is Affinity Fraud. Scams that target specific groups such as Christians, Jews, and Senior Citizens.

Affinity Fraud – What Is It?

Affinity Fraud. Sounds kind of exotic, and it may sound familiar but you are not sure. So what is Affinity Fraud and why should I be concerned about it? Legitimate questions, and here's why you need to know what it is and why you should be concerned.

Affinity Fraud simply means Investment scams that prey upon members of an identifiable group: seniors, Christians, Jews, Blacks, Hispanics, Asian, or Professional Groups. They can get you to become a victim as they claim to be "one" of you. They will tell you that your group is special because the investment is only available to members of your group.

One of the major scams that was going around specifically targeted the illegal alien community, because they knew these people would not go to the authorities and complain when they lose their money.

Earlier I mentioned that Christians, Senior Citizens and Jews were targeted, and now you know why. Because there are so many different types of these investment scams used to target the affinity groups, I am going to provide you the headlines of scams that were affinity groups who were the target of the scams. It will also demonstrate how easy it was to fool people into falling for these scams. The dollar amounts will astound you, at least they should. Here are just a small synopsis sampling of the types of affinity fraud and the losses involved:

TARGETING CHRISTIANS:

Randall W. Harding sang in the choir at Crossroads Christian Church in Corona, Calif., and donated part of his conspicuous wealth to its ministries. In his business dealings, he underscored his faith by naming his investment firm JTL, or "Just the Lord." Pastors and churchgoers alike entrusted their money to him. By the time Harding was unmasked as a fraud, he and his partners had stolen more than $50 million from their clients, and Crossroads became yet another cautionary tale in what investigators say is a worsening problem plaguing the nation's churches.

Lambert Vander Tuig, a member of Saddleback Church in Lake Forest Calif., ran a real estate scam that bilked investors out of $52 million, the Securities and Exchange Commission says. His salesmen presented themselves as faithful Christians and distributed copies of "The Purpose Driven Life," by Saddleback pastor Rick Warren. According to the SEC. Warren and his church had no knowledge of Vander Tuig's activities, says the SEC. Lambert Vander Tuig, Jonathan Carman, Mark Sostak, Scott Yard, Soren Svendsen, and Robert Waldman were charged in a civil case by the SEC, and criminal charges of fraud were filed against all six in the $52 Million dollar Ponzi scam by the Office of the California Attorney General.

At Daystar Assembly of God Church in Prattville, AL., a congregant persuaded church leaders and others to invest about $3 million in real estate a few years ago, promising some profits would go toward building a megachurch. The Daystar Assembly was swindled and lost its building. Nancilu Carpenter, Donald Cayton, Leonard Miller, William Till, Elaine Jenkins Turner and David Wayne Gordan were sentenced by the Honorable Ben Fuller, Circuit Judge for the Nineteenth Judicial Circuit, as a result of charges surrounding financial activities involving the proposed expansion of the former Daystar Assembly of God located in Prattville, Alabama.

And in a dramatically broader scam, leaders of Greater Ministries International, based in Tampa, Fla., defrauded thousands of people of half a billion dollars by promising to double money on investments that ministry officials said were blessed by God. Several of the con men were sentenced in 2001 to more than a decade each in prison.

Gene Robert Little, 62, a Fort Collins man has been arrested in connection with an alleged Ponzi scheme involving millions of dollars in investments from Northern Coloradans, Colorado Attorney General John Suthers and Securities Commissioner Fred Joseph said Wednesday. The indictment alleges that Little, through his company Managed Cash Flow, solicited more than $11 million in investments from more than 300 Coloradans between 2002 and 2006. Little allegedly promised investors returns of 15 percent to 20 percent. He found at least some of his investors through connections with local churches, including Timberline in Fort Collins and Christ Community in Greeley.

Churchgoers in as many as 10 states are investing in a company that some were told is worth $170 billion with assets around the world. Yet its business address is a Scottsdale post office box and state and federal officials are investigating its owners. At least one pastor, church elders and congregation members in Avondale and Chandler are among those who have put money into Nakami Chi Group Ministries International. The nonprofit company promises to fund Christian charities while paying investors 24 percent annual returns. Edward Purvis was indicted on 43 counts of fraud and theft in the Ponzi scheme, along with his wife Maureen and Gary Wolfe. January 23, 2009: In addition, Corporation Commission unanimously voted to sanction Chandler residents Edward A. Purvis and wife Maureen Purvis, Gregg Wolfe and their company, Nakami Chi Group Ministries International in one of the largest affinity fraud cases in Arizona since the Baptist Foundation. The Arizona Corporate Commission ordered over $11 million in restitution and $250, 000 in administrative penalties.

A U.S. District Court jury in Minneapolis found Forest Lake preacher Neulan Midkiff guilty on all 21 counts of mail and wire fraud and tax evasion. Midkiff founded Shiloh Church in Forest Lake after moving to Minnesota in 1994. He named himself "apostle" of the church and named his wife "proph-etess." Midkiff, 66, got many of his friends and neighbors involved in an Atlanta company called Horizon Enterprise, which promised high returns on an overseas banking deal but was actually a pyramid scheme that took in as much as $390 million. The scam paid investors "interest" using their own principal or money from new investors. He also ran offshoots, Central Financial Services and Joshua Tree Group, that scammed 519 people from Minnesota and Louisiana of $30 million.

Tri Energy's investors had something in common. Many were Mormons and born-again Christians who shared dreams and prayers on nightly conference calls. They vowed to use the profits for charitable works and kept raising funds, at times taking out second mortgages, draining retirement accounts, and recruiting relatives. All were victims in a $50 Million dollar scam to sell gold bullion.

In May 2005, the U.S. Securities and Exchange Commission obtained a temporary restraining order against Jones and his partners, Robert Jennings, an associate pastor at the New Life Fellowship Church in Perris, California, and Arthur Simburg, a former marketing representative for sporting-goods manufacturer Puma AG. Jones, a native of Nigeria, and Jennings, 59, were later convicted in federal court in Los Angeles on charges of mail, wire, and securities fraud. Jennings was sentenced last November to 12 years in prison, and Jones got 20 years in April. Both men have filed notices that they intend to appeal. Simburg, 64, who pleaded guilty and cooperated with prosecutors, received a nine- year sentence.

The final defendant has pleaded guilty in a fraud case linked to the collapse of the Baptist Foundation of Arizona, one of the nation's largest nonprofit bankruptcy filings. About 11,000 mostly elderly investors lost almost $600 million as a result. Lawrence Dwain Hoover, 71, who served two decades on the foundation's board, faces up to 12 1/2 years in prison when he's sentenced in late November. In July, a Maricopa County jury found former foundation president William Crotts and ex-BFA general counsel Thomas Grabinski guilty of three counts of fraud and one count of illegally conducting an enterprise.

Charges of 174 counts of mail fraud, money-laundering and transporting stolen goods were brought against "3 Hebrew Boys" — Joseph Brunson, Tim McQueen, and Tony Pough. They were accused of defrauding participants in a bogus debt-relief "ministry," and were found guilty on all charges. The scam was targeted at churchgoers and members of the military from South Carolina and North Carolina, and from other states.

James Paul Lewis, Jr., Financial Advisory Consultants, who had more than 5,200 clients across the country. He obtained his clients from fellow LDS churchgoers, which included professional athletes and at least one movie star. The SEC says his accounts totaled $813 Million Dollars. Barry Minkow said, "It is the longest-running Ponzi scheme in history, and based on the mutual fund that didn't exist."

TARGETING JEWS:

Two New Jersey men were charged for their role in a $200 million Ponzi scheme that targeted Orthodox Jews, according to the Federal Bureau of Investigation and U.S. prosecutors. Eliyahu Weinstein, 35, was charged with orchestrating a real-estate investment fraud to dupe fellow Orthodox Jews in

New Jersey, New York, Florida, California, and abroad, U.S. Attorney Paul Fishman said today in a statement. Vladimir Siforov, 43, also was charged in the scheme. By using "lies, threats, deliberate misrepresentations and even counterfeit checks, forged or created multiple deeds, transfer documents, corporate documents and other financial records, and convinced his 'investors' to loan or invest hundreds of millions of dollars to acquire interests in properties" that were never purchased." Weinstein and Siforov "exploited the close community ties of the Orthodox Jewish community for one goal: to steal money through an elaborate real estate and Ponzi scheme," Michael B. Ward, special agent in charge of the FBI's office in Newark, New Jersey, said in a statement.

A Ponzi schemer who targeted Orthodox Jewish communities from New York to Chicago pleaded guilty yesterday to bilking investors of about $225 million. Steven Byers admitted he lied to investors of his now-defunct real estate fund WexTrust Capital LLC., and its roughly 120 spin-offs. Byers admitted he used new investors' money to pay earlier investors, and then concocted statements that lied about how much money was being made. He and WexTrust co-founder, Joseph Shereshevsky, were arrested in 2008. Shereshevsky has denied committing any crimes.

A Massachusetts investment manager was arrested for running a multimillion-dollar Ponzi scheme that preyed heavily on elderly Jewish country club members. The FBI arrested Richard Elkinson, 76, in Mississippi, according to the Boston Globe, for running a $29 million affinity scheme, which uses personal relationships and social networks to get close to potential victims. Many of his investors were referred to Elkinson through RossFialkow Capital Partners. Many were elderly Jewish members of the Belmont Country Club in Massachusetts.

DELRAY BEACH–Florida Chief Financial Officer Alex Sink has revoked the license of a south Florida agent and permanently banned him from the insurance business in Florida for using his insurance license to exploit elderly Jewish Floridians. Leighton David Applefeld, 66, owned and operated Focus Financial Services, Inc. in Delray Beach. In February, the Department of Financial Services filed an 18-count administrative complaint against Applefeld alleging, among other things, that he preyed on elderly Jewish consumers, through religious affinity, to engender their trust and sell them inappropriate insurance products that paid high commissions. In lieu of fighting the administrative charges against him, Applefeld agreed to the revocation of his insurance license, and further agreed to be permanently banned from the insurance business in Florida.

SCOTT ROTHSTEIN, South Florida Ponzi scheme mastermind sentenced to 50 years in prison on Wednesday June 9, just a day before his 48th birthday for an investment fraud of more than $1.2 billion. South Florida Ponzi scheme involved attracting investors with big interest rates from the sale of confidential legal settlements that were nothing but fiction, as well as fake bank statements showing money in accounts that didn't exist. In his sentencing, Judge Cohn called Scott Rothstein's investment scam a 'tsunami' that he created through his law firm, Rothstein Rosenfeldt Adler P.A, his political connections, his charities and ultimately, by forging the signatures of judges in a legal case between auto magnate Ed Morse and an interior decorator.

Michael S. Goldberg, 39 of Wethersfield, Conn, told clients he invested in "diamond contracts" and told clients he invested in "distressed assets from JP Morgan Chase Bank, but were nonexistent diamond contracts and nonexistent Chase deals. Instead he was running a $100 Million dollar Ponzi, and paying returns from his Ponzi operation. "When an investor questioned Goldberg about his business relationships, either with Chase or with any other company, he often created false documents and other items to induce investors to believe that his business relationships were legitimate, including inventories and/or manifests, contracts, business checks, bank statements, business cards and company identification cards," prosecutors said.

And of course I would be remiss if I did not mention Bernard Madoff and the estimated $65 Billion dollar hedge fund Ponzi Scheme. Bernard Madoff has now become the poster boy for the Ponzi scheme. From now on all Ponzi's will be compared to him.

TARGETING SENIORS:

Here is just a small list of Seniors being scammed by their fellow seniors:

A Louisiana man has been charged in a 64-count indictment with operating a $20 million Ponzi scheme that fleeced retirees, federal prosecutors said today. He "lured his potential victims through advertisements in the local daily newspapers in New Orleans, Baton Rouge and Hammond by promising rates of returns that were higher than market rates for CDs or U.S. Treasury Bills, prosecutors said. Among the words Pizzolato used to lure investors into a false sense of security were "guaranteed", "safe", "conservative", "insured", and "no-risk," prosecutors said. Scott was accused today of telling investors their funds would be used to purchase or finance the purchase of high-speed commercial printers that would be sold to third-party buyers at a profit.

Tom Petters, accused of operating a $3.65 billion Ponzi scheme by deceiving investors into thinking they were financing his company's purchase of electronics that later would be sold to Wal-Mart and other huge retailers.

Michael Goldberg "falsely represented to prospective investors that he and his company, AUG, were in the business of liquidating assets held by JP Morgan Chase (formerly Chase Manhattan Bank), and that GOLDBERG induced investors to provide him and AUG funds by promising and paying up to 20 percent quarterly returns," prosecutors said.

A Georgia attorney, Gregory Bartko, 56, representing defendants in the alleged "Billionaire Boys Club" Ponzi scheme in Michigan has been indicted in North Carolina on charges he ran his own securities-fraud scheme.

Kenneth Kenitzer, 66, of Pleasanton has become the most recent senior citizen to face significant jail time for his actions in a Ponzi and affinity fraud scheme. The California Ponzi fleeced investors and churchgoers out of at least $40 million, authorities said.

Julia Ann Schmidt, the 68-year-old alleged Ponzi schemer from Texas, posed as an investment adviser using the name of Fortis Investments, a famous European brand with U.S. reach.

Eugene D. Miley, 58, of Beaver, defrauded credit unions in Armstrong, Westmoreland and Luzerne counties out of $2 million in a Ponzi scheme, said Pennsylvania Attorney General Tom Corbett. Miley served as a financial broker for clients, "offering to locate and purchase high-interest-rate certificates of deposit (CDs) for those institutions," prosecutors said.

Michael J. Morris, 29, and William T. Perkins, 54, were charged and arrested, amid allegations they fleeced 21 Michigan churches out of $660,000 in a Ponzi and affinity fraud scheme in which pastors were duped into giving a leasing company access to church bank accounts.

A Florida man, Nilton Rossoni, 50, has been convicted in a scheme carried out on eBay, one of the most famous websites and brands in the world. Rossoni created "more than 260 different eBay accounts" using aliases "or the real names and address of unsuspecting individuals." Rossoni gathered money for more than 5,500 items but never shipped them. He netted $717,000.

Richard M. Harkless, 65, operated the MX Factors Ponzi scheme earlier this decade. Prosecutors said he began to hide money offshore when the scheme was on the verge of discovery by authorities bilked seniors out of $60 Million Dollars. MX Factors positioned as a government-guaranteed loans program were promised returns of up to 14 percent every 60 to 90 days.

John W. Heath, 81, was sentenced to 127 years in prison for his targeting more than 1,800 San Diego area seniors in his $187 Million Dollar Ponzi scheme.

Reed E. Slatkin, 54, confessed to running a $254 Million dollar Ponzi scheme that targeted senior citizens. He preyed on the sick, dying, and the most vulnerable, accepting $7 Million dollars 3 months before his Ponzi scheme collapsed. He was using the money to support his lavish lifestyle of airplanes, luxury cars, real estate, artwork, and gold.

Jeffrey Gordon Butler first aided his clients with their wills and trusts, then he helped himself to their money. Butler was found guilty of running an investment Ponzi scheme of approximately $11 Million dollars from his senior citizen clients. He was just sentenced to 80 years in prison.

EVEN SOPHISTICATED LAW ENFORCEMENT OFFICERS GET SCAMMED BY PONZI SCHEME:

Hundreds of experienced law enforcement officers, including FBI agents, have been taken for tens of millions of dollars from a man who committed suicide two months ago after his Ponzi scheme was discovered. In this case more than 1,000 working and retired law enforcement officers bought into a pitch that they would earn every year an 8 to 10 percent tax free return. Kenneth Wayne McLeod, 48, for more than 20 years, he gave seminars explaining how to get the most out of government retirement benefits, drawing rave reviews from the FBI, Drug Enforcement Administration, Immigration and Customs Enforcement, and U.S. Customs and Border Protection employees he was hired to teach. McLeod signed up audience members for his own money management firm, F&S Asset Management Group, which oversaw $43 million for 1,100 people, almost all of them current or retired law enforcement. McLeod lured them with what he called his "special fund," government bonds that he promised would return 8percent to 10percent interest annually, tax-free. After his office was raided by SEC Investigators, he broke down and admitted for two decades he had been running a Ponzi scheme.

As you can see, affinity fraud is alive and well within the specified target groups. Now there are many more examples I could provide, but these three categories represent the largest target groups. The most shocking trend of late has been the number of senior citizens who are scamming their fellow senior citizens. Not only that, but also some who are running these scams are professional people seniors have put their trust in such as: Attorneys, Accountants, Financial Planners, Insurance Agents, Real Estate Agents, Pastors, Rabbi's, Radio Hosts, Retired Police Officer's, and Stock Brokers. Not only do you now have to check out your investments, but also you have to check out your professional advisor to make sure they are not going to rob you too. We are all vulnerable, as you have seen.

If any professional is offering any type of investment opportunity, they must be a licensed broker with FINRA, and the investment must be registered with the SEC. So make sure you see their broker number and registration number with the SEC before even considering investing.

Another illegal program that became a hot commodity that spread like wildfire was the Pay-To-Click/Auto-Surf programs. The landscape is littered with the failed remains of these scams, or from those shut-down by the feds. Yet they seem to keep re-inventing themselves as having worked out all the previous problems with the failed programs, but in reality is only putting a new dress on the same pig. Here's the Pay-To-Click/Auto-Surf Scam.

Pay-To-Click/Auto-Surf Programs

The concept behind this investment program is you will join a company that offers to sell you advertising called ad packs/ad views/page impressions (or whatever) for you to promote your business website on their rotator of businesses. The premise is your website will be seen by thousands of people. Not only are you buying ad packages to advertise your business website, but also they will pay you a rebate of 1% per day until you have received a return of 125%/150%/110% of your ad package cost. They also offer you a referral fee of 10% for every person you sign-up to join this program, and by displaying your business website on their rotator, you will receive increased revenue from people buying your products. The major problem with advertising through these companies is that they cannot provide you targeted advertising. If you own a business that is not an MLM or Network Marketing Company, you are wasting your money. You need target marketing, and these programs cannot provide it. Your ad is seen by anyone no matter where he or she are located. They are not going to patronize your business if they are not located in your area. Of course selling advertising is just the guise they use to get you to join. What they are really selling you is to make their company your business, and to get a return on your investment.

Each auto-surf program develops its own unique payment plan for their members, but in reality they are not that different. What is also true is the landscape of this industry is littered with failed ad-surf companies either by self-destruction or those who have been shut-down by the authorities for selling unregistered securities, wire fraud, bank fraud, money laundering, and being a Ponzi scheme.

ASD Cash Generator, hereafter called ASD, was nothing more than a compilation of PhoenixSurf, 12DP (12DailyPro) and CEP (Colon End Parenthesis Trust); all raided and shut-down by the government. ASD started within months of the closure of 12DP. It seems the fact that the exact same type of businesses were raided and shut-down by the feds was lost on Andy Bowdoin in launching ASD.

One of the marketing strategies of ASD that set it apart from the other failed auto-surf programs before it was the rally's they held around the country. To make the attendance even greater, they promised all who signed-up in ASD at these rally's their sponsor and themselves would receive a matching bonus of 150% rebate instead of the standard 125% rebate. People were lined up to sign-up in ASD in droves even before they had attended the presentation. Andy also declared that ASD would make One Hundred Thousand Millionaires, among other outlandish claims; but the people believed it.

Another one of their pitches was if you didn't have a business to advertise, they would provide one for you. You had senior citizens in their 70's and 80's putting their life savings into ASD that had no clue how a computer worked, let alone have a business to advertise on the Internet. But the claim was ASD was legal and not an illegal pyramid scheme or a Ponzi.

One of the biggest reasons people rushed to join ASD was a Legality Statement that was presented by the corporate attorney, Robert Garner, vouching for the legitimacy of ASD. Here is Mr. Garner's Legality Statement:

LEGALITY STATEMENT

Presented by Mr. Robert Garner, Attorney at Law,

Chief Legal Counsel for Ad Surf Daily, Inc.

Garner Law Office – P.O. Box 13002 – Greensboro - NC – 27415 – USA

INTRODUCTION

My name is Robert Garner, and I am an attorney and the principle owner of the Garner Law Office in Greensboro, North Carolina. At our Law Office we specialize in corporate, business and real estate law, and my firm represents Ad Surf Daily, Inc., or ASD, which is Andy Bowdoin's company that operates the Ad Cash Generator business opportunity.

To give you some of my background as an attorney, I am a graduate of the Law School at the University of North Carolina at Chapel Hill, and I've had thirty years experience as a North Carolina licensed attorney. I have handled everything from first degree murder cases to million dollar construction litigation. But for the past twenty years, I have primarily represented corporations and security houses, such as stock brokerage firms and investment firms.

Our work includes the handling of public stock offerings, negotiating complex mergers and acquisitions, and the preparation of filings for the Securities and Exchange Commission, also known as the SEC. In case you don't know, the SEC is a regulatory branch of the US Government created by Congress to protect investors from fraud and other abuses.

In addition to myself, we have other attorneys in our offices who are dedicated to this work with Andy and his company, and who are available at any time to deal with issues as they arise. We are working daily to advance the business plans of Andy's entire organization, and we are moving forward in a number of positive directions which will benefit everyone involved.

LEGALITY CONCERNS

Now, I want to address the concern that new ASD members sometimes have in the area of the legality of the Ad Cash Generator opportunity. And for the record, I can say that there is no litigation, no threatened litigation, or even any inquiries from any regulatory body about ASD or the Ad Cash Generator opportunity.

Everyone at my law firm understands Andy's sincere commitment to honesty and integrity in all aspects of his company, and we have given those values the highest level of importance in all our activities as his legal counsel. For the past 2 years now, Andy has directed us to ensure that his company is structurally sound today and tomorrow and far into the future. My staff and I are dedicated to Andy's vision that his company will continue to rapidly grow bigger and stronger, and will continue to be an industry leader in Internet advertising in the years to come.

LEGALITY OVERVIEW

Now, here is an overview of what ASD and the Ad Cash Generator income opportunity program are doing from a legal viewpoint:

ASD and the Ad Cash Generator opportunity provide businesses a way to advertise on the Internet. It allows them to purchase page views, where their ads can be seen by the general public. At this time, Ad Cash Generator is offering rebates to purchasers of advertising. These rebates function something like "loss leaders" in that advertisers are presented a way to earn their money back, plus a little more, in addition to having their ads viewed on the Internet. If you are not familiar with this business term "loss leader", it is when a product or service is sold at a very low price or at a loss for the purpose of attracting customers to a retail store.

Not everyone qualifies for the rebates, but for those who do participate, it is a great opportunity for them to expose their Websites to the public, and earn back some of the cost. I should tell you that like all rebates, this offer may be withdrawn at some time in the future, and the opportunity will be gone. However, the special offers will be honored for all who do participate at this time.

These ASD programs are open to everybody. ASD had a program to allow businesses to place ads on the ASD site for viewing by the general public without cost. For others who are seeking wider exposure, there are "ad packages" available for purchase which will guarantee greater numbers of page views, as selected by the advertiser. It is for those people that a rebate program is available now, to recover their cost, and perhaps earn some additional money. As ASD grows and develops, this program may change and improve as well.

COMPANY OPERATIONS

Now, I would like to go over some legal and operational information about ASD as a company.

ASD is incorporated, pays state, federal and all other taxes, and complies with all laws and regulations that apply to it. It provides its contact information, including its physical location, on the Internet. It has customer service representatives who are responsive to customer calls. The customer service representatives are not offshore, they are right here in the United States. To provide even better customer support, ASD has implemented a "ticket" system to allow inquiries via its website, and answers every one within 24 hours, Monday through Friday. The goal is to have zero customer complaints.

In addition, ASD is continuing the expensive work of improving back office operations, so that everything will run more smoothly for everyone. And, as I stated before, there are many other exciting things coming in the future that will benefit everyone involved with the ASD income opportunities.

ASD and its related companies are not selling stock, nor are they seeking investors. Should any of the related companies elect to do so in the future, strict adherence to SEC and state regulations would be observed. At this stage, a stock offering to the general public, in compliance with SEC regulations, is at best only in the talking phase. There are no concrete plans for this right now.

If ASD or its related companies were to offer shares of stock, they would be required to file a registration statement with the SEC. If ASD, or anyone, anywhere were to offer a "security," which is defined as an investment opportunity, to US citizens, the offering would need to be first approved by the SEC before being legal. The ASD rebate program is designed to respect these regulations. It is not an investment opportunity, and should not be considered as such. ASD is seeking to build up its base of subcontractors who will continue to sell Internet advertising for them, even after the rebate program ends and is replaced with something even more exciting and beneficial. ASD also wants to acquire information about companies that will continue to purchase advertising on the Internet in the future, and ASD is willing to pay for that information through the rebate program.

Because of the rebate program, some people have asked if ASD or the Ad Cash Generator income opportunity is a "Ponzi" scheme or a pyramid. A Ponzi scheme and/or a pyramid are illegal, because they use money from new investors to pay the first investors in the scheme their promised returns. When the base of the pyramid stops growing, the pyramid collapses. While ASD commits a portion of its future revenues to pay rebates, it does not guarantee a return, and the time it takes to earn rebates is affected by the revenue stream in the future. Not everyone elects to participate in the rebate program, and not everyone will earn rebates.

ASD's Ad Cash Generator business model is not dependent on a base that continues to expand. Plus, ASD is developing other revenue sources constantly. Even more important, the rebates are fixed, and will allow the participants to only earn a set amount, and that amount is based on performance. There is no continuing obligation to pay returns to infinity, as in illegal pyramid programs. Because of these major differences, the Ad Cash Generator business opportunity is not an illegal "Ponzi" scheme or pyramid, and it is not in violation of any SEC laws or regulations.

As the founder and president of ASD, Andy envisions a day in the near future when the company will operate as a premier distributor of Internet advertising, utilizing the information now being acquired to market its services. We understand that Andy's goal is to follow the example of other broad based companies such as Amway and Avon, and to use the methods they developed to become a recognized leader in providing Internet marketing services.

FURTHER LEGAL QUESTIONS

If anyone has legal questions about the Ad Cash Generator opportunity, I have provided this Legality Statement on the ASD Website that you are now reading. If you cannot find answers to your questions here, you should contact the staff at ASD, or submit a ticket for a written response. For more complex legal or regulatory questions, we ask that you have your attorney contact us for more detailed discussions, and we are happy to take such calls at 336-621-3890. Note: We will only take these legality question calls from licensed attorneys, so please have your attorney call us, not you.

In closing I want to assure you that as a licensed attorney for the past 30 years, I know there is no such thing as a free lunch, meaning you can get paid money for doing nothing in exchange. But, at the same time, I do believe that opportunity still exists, and that steady work and dedication can pay off. We know that ASD is committed to creating an environment where these opportunities can be found, opportunities to earn the money necessary for the challenging economic times ahead and for those who want to achieve even higher long term goals to live a life with much more financial freedom and security for them and their families.

We wish everyone involved with the Ad Cash Generator great success, and we will do our part to help make it happen.

Robert Garner

Based on this statement, people just blindly accepted what was said with no questions asked. But if you stop and think when you are reading the letter, and ask yourself some basic questions; you begin to see the holes in the statement and its validity.

Please note that Mr. Garner uses a P.O. Box for his law firm. While it is true that many law firms do have a P.O. Box, they use their street address on major correspondence. Also note the pitch is not for you to advertise your business, but to make ASD your business. In doing a search about Mr. Garner and his law firm, I discovered the following pieces of information that tended to raise serious doubts about Mr. Garner's securities background and his law firm.

I did a search of the greater Greensboro Yellow Pages to see if Mr. Garner and his prestigious securities law firm was listed. In the Greensboro Yellow Pages under Securities & Investment Law, of the 11 firms listed, Mr. Garner's firm is not listed. Because Mr. Garner is ASD's corporate attorney, I then looked under the Corporation & Partnership listings in the Greensboro Yellow Pages. Of the 240 firms listed, Mr. Garner's firm is not listed. I then checked under the Business Law listings, and out of the 171 firms listed, Mr. Garner' firm is not listed. The Greensboro Yellow Pages does not have a listing for Real Estate Attorney's, which I found quite odd since he claims such distinction. On another note, most major brokerage houses have in-house council and when they do hire outside council, it is from a prestigious law firm, of which Mr. Garner's firm did not approach this level of distinction. The phone number he provided was listed to three entities: Turning Wheels, Inc.; Tsunami Holdings; and his home phone number. I could not find a listing for his law firm, or a street address; but only the P.O. Box listing. I was never able to establish that he had other attorney's in his firm, but instead worked out of his home. Another major tell-tale problem was he is not listed in the Martindale-Hubbell Law Directory. In essence Mr. Garner seemed to have embellished his credentials significantly from the little bit of information I uncovered on him. It remains a mystery why a professional attorney would even issue this legality statement, which would later to be proved totally false. He is a member of the North Carolina Bar Association.

To give a better illustration of how these programs work, I will use the format used by ASD. I am going to use their marketing material to illustrate how they work; and give an analysis of each section as we go along. This is from their sales material:

AdSurfDaily, Inc. (ASD) is an advertising company, specializing in a unique approach to sending traffic to websites.

Advertisers can buy advertising packages on ASD. Advertisers can earn 125% of their money back by viewing other websites on the ASD web site, simply by viewing up to 12-24 web sites daily for 15 seconds each.

ASD pays up to 10% in commissions to existing advertisers for referring other businesses to buy advertising.

This new approach to Internet advertising has businesses of all sizes, from small home based businesses to large corporations such as Google, Starbucks, Kodak, etc., joining ASD.

ASD not only makes money from selling ad time across their network, they also generate income from other sources. Understand that ASD has great flexibility in how they allocate their revenue because it is generated from multiple sources. 50% of total revenue generated by the following sources is re-distributed daily:

- *Ad Surf Daily- Advertising Revenue*
- *Ad Surf Daily- Major Corporate Advertising*
- *Ad Surf Daily- Ad Placement Company*
- *Ad Surf Daily- E-book Sales*
- *Ad Surf Daily- Membership Revenue*
- *Ad Surf Daily- Sister Advertising Company*
- *Media Player*
- *National Visa Debit Cards*
- *In Flight Magazine- Advertising revenue from the promotion of the ASD service which is seen by over 20 million travelers on 11 major airlines per months*

Other revenue sources are in development...

My analysis of these statements:

Contrary to what ASD claimed, they did not have any unique approach to sending traffic to websites. 12DailyPro, Phoenix-Surf and CEP all did the very same thing.

The only difference in what ASD paid versus the other ad-surf programs. This is usually the only distinctive difference between ad-surf companies.

Every ad-surf company pays referral fees, and the standard is 10%.

This last claim was a total lie. There were no major corporations such as Google, Starbucks, Kodak, etc. advertising with ASD. While they did display these companies, and others, logos on their website, none of them were advertisers with ASD. The other revenue streams they claimed were either nonexistent or were totally fabricated. The only product ASD had was the selling of their ad packs.

OVERVIEW SUMMARY

Ad Surf Daily has developed a totally unique approach to Internet advertising. ASD is the future of advertising. Internet advertising is the fastest growing industry in the history of world commerce. Having your business buried millions deep in Google searches, or having to pay a large fee to get on the first page is a losing battle. Why not simply participate in a business opportunity that encourages participation of the advertisers through rebate incentives? When existing members are enjoying a great income generating and advertising experience, referring other businesses to ASD will simply take care of itself. This is the powerful business model Ad Surf Daily has created and why they are seeing unheard of growth.

Can you imagine the stress that would be eliminated if the rent or lease on your office or store was paid for every month with these rebates? Or income was generated for a new company car? Or how about generating enough income with ASD to allow you to leave your business and retire. You all are truly in the midst of a life changing opportunity.

Now we are getting to the real business of ASD. They sold you ASD was the best way for you to advertise your existing business on the Internet, but their real goal is for you to quit your business and make ASD your business. They do this by paying you a 125% rebate of your ad packs, and of course your 10% referral fee, where in a very short period of time your rebates and referral fees are making you more money than your business (in spite of ASD's claim your advertising your business on their website will generate significant new revenue for your business); thus you will want to quit your business and make ASD your business. Up until now, they have hidden this fact from you, and here it is just used as a toss away line to set the stage for convincing you the need to make ASD your business. There was a Q&A section in their marketing material, and I want to address the first question asked:

Q: I have heard some people say this is a pyramid business?

A: A pyramid business or scheme depends on recruiting people to join your business, no product or service is sold. The ONLY money coming in is from new recruits. ASD sells Internet advertising, for every dollar worth of advertising you buy you receive 1 unique viewer to the website of your choice for a minimum of 15 seconds. You are not investing, you are buying advertising. With ASD you can join for free and get people to view your website from day one. If you want to make money, all you have to do is buy a minimum of $10 worth of advertising and the first day you are making money. You never have to tell anyone what you are doing, there is no recruiting or selling. However if you want to sell Internet advertising, because that is what ASD sells, Internet advertising, you can, and receive referral commissions.

Contrary to what ASD claimed, the rebates came from ASD profits. This is a return on investment. Calling it ad packs does not change the fact you were investing in ASD. The Supreme Court of the United States, held "that the definition of a security includes an investment contract, which is "a contract, transaction, or scheme whereby a person invests his money in a common enterprise and is led to expect profits solely from the efforts of the promoter or third party...Designating such instruments as "loans" does not alter their legal status as securities." SEC v. W.J. Howey Co., et. al, 328 U.S. 293, 66 S. Ct.1100, 90 L.Ed. 1244 (1946).

Not matter what you call it, ad packs were a security. When the Secret Service raided ASD in August of 08, and froze all the assets, it was done on the basis that ASD was operating as a Ponzi scheme over the Internet. All the bank accounts (at least 10) frozen were in the name of Andy Bowdoin, Sole Proprietor, DBA AdSurfDaily, not in the ASD Cash Generator corporate bank account.

As mentioned earlier from the sales brochure provided by ASD, they claimed:

CORPORATIONS ADVERTISING WITH ASD

Not only are there over 75,000 small businesses advertising with ASD, but now major corporations are as well. Remember, a part of the daily rebate comes from the revenue corporations pay to advertise with ASD. The following are just a few of these companies:

Google   Kodak   Tilly's   Callaway Golf   Quiznos Sub   Starbucks
Macys   American Airlines   Discovery   Gamefly   dishNetwork   Pespsi
NBC   USA Today   Free Credit-Report.com   Rhapsody   Toshiba
Farmers Insurance   StubHub   Fandango   Priceline.com

These companies and their logos were shown on the ASD Website, and ASD claimed they were corporate advertisers. None of these companies were advertising with ASD.

One of the prominent pitches made by ASD was the biography of the founder, Andy Bowdoin. This is the biography provided for him:

Biography of Mr. Andy Bowdoin:

Andy started his career working with Dale Carnegie, world famous author of **How to Win Friends and Influence People**. Andy taught Dale Carnegie Courses in the early sixties training hundreds of thousands of sales professionals.

He then he went on to work directly with the notorious Napoleon Hill author of **Think and Grow Rich**, one of the best-selling books of all time. It was with Napoleon Hill, Andy learned many life changing business principles that would help him succeed over the next 40 years.

Next, Andy had huge success expanding a 60-minute dry cleaning franchise throughout the Southeast and Midwest. Then Andy developed a company that sold wireless communication franchises throughout the US. He saw cell phones as a growing industry that had tremendous growth potential. This is before anyone knew what cell phones were and weighed 15 pounds. Once the industry matured, he sold his company to Bell South, which was bought by Cingular, now AT&T.

Andy recognized the growing use of credit cards. He started a company to market credit card processing for merchants and soon was in stores all over the country. As we all have seen, you can now use credit cards at practically any business.

In 1999, Andy discovered a need for GPS Tracking for fleet vehicles and GPS Tech was created. This technology saved companies hundreds of thousands of dollars and was a huge success.

In 2006, Andy again saw a new opportunity, the need for a new way to deliver advertising to the masses and AdSurfDaily was born. He quickly assembled a team of associates who have joined with him to create what is quickly becoming the largest Internet advertising company in history.

As you can clearly see, Andy Bowdoin has had success in every company he has started, and is well respected in the global business community. In fact, AdSurfDaily President and CEO, Andy Bowdoin, was invited to Washington, D.C., in June, 2008, by United States President George Bush and Vice President Dick Cheney to receive the Medal of Distinction, at the White House. This is a very special honor for his service and leadership contributions in business.

Too bad none of it is true.

Here's the real biography of Andy Bowdoin:

In 1999, Andy did research and discovered a need for GPS Tracking for fleet vehicles and GPS Tech was created. GPS TECH, INC. was incorporated 03/26/2004, five years later than claimed. When the company was contacted, they had never heard of him.

Andy has trained thousands of salespeople during his career and started several companies. No mention that Andy from November 14, 1983 to September 14, 2007 has had 14 companies either dissolved voluntarily or were involuntarily dissolved.

Andy developed a company that sold wireless communication franchises throughout the U.S. and then started a company to market credit card processing for merchants. Perry Technology Corporation was "involuntarily dissolved 12/16/1981.

Andy has two prior felony convictions for selling unregistered securities, and is still making restitution from the last conviction. Quite the opposite of what is portrayed in his biography and told to the membership of ASD as Andy being this astute, honest businessman, and a man of integrity.

The Medal of Distinction is awarded to anyone who donates at least $2,500 to the Republican party. It had nothing to do with his "service, leadership, and contributions to business;" for if it did he would have never received it. He attended a dinner in Washington, DC at which there were more than 2,500 people in attendance, and more than 250 recipients of this medal.

Initially when ASD was raided and shut-down, over $53 Million dollars was frozen. ASD claimed it had liabilities of only $24+ Million, and therefore was not operating as a Ponzi. ASD requested an Emergency Evidentiary Hearing to show it was not operating as an illegal Ponzi.

ASD submitted a Balance Statement (unaudited), in an apparent effort to show that ASD was not a Ponzi because the seized funds were more than adequate to cover the cash-out balances of all the members; with millions to spare.   Yet in their filing of the emergency request for the Evidentiary Hearing, they claimed litigation lasting even three months will bankrupt ASD despite its supposed cash surplus.

According to its own records, as of July 31, 2008, ASD had on its books income from the sale of $100,888,592.23 worth of ad packages, but total assets of only $41,879,631.31. Even if only half of the so-called ads purchases came from individuals who participated in the surfing rebate program, ASD still needed more than $62,500,000 to fund the rebates it would owe those members for surfing. The judge denied ASD's request for all seized funds to be returned, and that ASD had failed to prove it was not operating as a Ponzi. Since this ruling was made, ASD has filed several appeals of the court's rulings, and these are now awaiting adjudication on the last appeal filed.

ASD actually began in October 2006 as Ad Surf Daily. Then in March 2007 it changed the name to ASD Cash Generator with its new website. It wasn't until the early part of 2008 that ASD exploded with growth and revenue until its closure August 1, 2008, and raid of August 5, 2008.

Since the demise of ASD, there have been numerous new auto-surf programs that have all claimed to have solved the problems of those programs that have gone before that collapsed or were shut down by the authorities. Just a few are: AVGA (Ad View Global Association), AGW (Ad Gate World), BAS (Biz Ad Splash); all of these were started by former ASD principals or employees of ASD; adventures4U, Megalido, Noobing, MrsVIP-VLane, and PaperlessAccess to name a few. They all have collapsed leaving millions stolen, and thousands of victims in their wake. Hopefully people are catching on they are illegal, and not to join these programs.

LET'S RECAP:

It makes no difference what you call it, ad packs, ad views, page impressions they are offering unregistered securities and it is illegal.

Every new auto-surf program claims it has worked the bugs out, or solved the problems of previously failed programs, or were shut-down by the authorities. Just a new dress on the same pig.

Don't just accept with blind faith the content of the biography of any of the Principal's. Check them out. Make sure what they say and claim is true.

Companies do not pay you in rebates more than the cost of the product. The reason companies, mainly in the cellular industry, give you rebates equal to the cost of the phone is because you have to sign-up for at least a two-year contract for their cellular services. It is not free as it seems to be. If you leave the program before the two years, your cost is triple what the cost of your "free" phone.

Joining such a company that cannot offer you targeted marketing is a total waste of your advertising dollars no matter how good it sounds. That is if you want to obtain customers for your business, not make this company your business.

They are not interested in your business, they are interested in one thing and one thing only...they want you to become one of them and make their company your business.

If a company is touting having received a prestigious award, check to make sure the award is real, and the honor in receiving it is real.

Remember: Verify, Verify, Verify

Next an Investment scam that primarily operated via E-mail, and in the late 90s to around 2004 was one of the more prevalent investment scams going. Since 2004, it has declined in frequency and in the amount of money stolen. Like all scams, they flourish then they seem to disappear for a short while; but then they come back in force. I believe it is about time for this scam to make a comeback given the current economic instability and people being susceptible to financial desperation. This is the Penny Stock Pump and Dump Scam.

Penny Stock Pump & Dump

Penny stocks are what is known in the trades as "Pink Sheet" stocks. They are called this because they are listed on pink paper and sent to all the brokerage houses. They are not listed on any exchange, as they are too small in assets to be listed, and they cannot afford the listing fees for the major exchanges. They are for all practical purposes, a sub-set of the OTC market. They also do not require all the financial reporting requirements that the OTC stocks require. Basically you invest in these at your own risk. The margins are very thin as well as the volume of shares traded daily. The bid and ask price is arbitrary, and to be honest most of the time make no rhyme or reason for the bid and ask price shown. The price is whatever the buyer and seller are willing to agree on a sale price. This makes them a license to steal.

Here's how this scam works. Someone sees a dormant, but active listing for a company. This simply means the registration is current, but there is no trading in the stock. A shell company is formed, and then they do a reverse merger. They acquire this listed company, and then after the merger, they announce a new company and new stock symbol for the company. They then begin having press releases made about the new company, its goals, its market, and of course how they will soon become successful enough to be listed on the OTC market.

Because they are not known and do not trade on any trading board, they have to generate interest in their company to get people to buy their shares. That is the purpose of all the press releases, which they paid for by the way and they wrote. They then obtain an E-mail list, and they begin their pitch. They announce in their E-mail they have had this major break-through in technology, a major new contract will be signed, you get the drift of the type of stories they will make up to get you excited about the company. Then they tell you of the wonderful opportunity that you have by buying their stock now before the significant price increase.

To make you think there really is interest in their company, they will have made a significant amount of trades in their stock with slightly increasing prices for the illusion of growth and interest in the stock. What you don't know is all this stock trading is among the people who own the shares in the company, not from outside investors. You are the one they are targeting to be the outside investor.

Then the really big news is that with all these exciting things happening they believe the stock will double, triple, or even quadruple in price in the next few weeks when this news is announced to the public. But you can get it now for the current trading price of (they put a price here that is higher than the last traded price that they have driven up 10 times its actual price if not more), but it requires a minimum number of shares to be bought (usually 1,000, but can be 5,000 or 10,000-depends on the price they want you to pay).

Of course in this E-mail they give you other press-releases they have bought and wrote to convey to you this new opportunity is real. They even provide you a link to a broker if you don't already have one. So you decide this is a great opportunity, and you can see you doubling or tripling your money very quickly, so you buy.

When the date arrives they were to announce this new deal or technology break-through, something happens to delay the announcement. They assure you this is just a temporary setback, but it won't be much longer until the announcement will be made. But hey, it won't be long now until you will get your return on your investment. Then once again something mysteriously happens to delay the announcement again, or the company just folds leaving you holding worthless stock. If they don't fold, they will be gracious enough to buy back your stock, but of course at two cents on the dollar.

There was one case many years ago, where a company that pulled this stunt, announced a reverse merger with another shell company, formed a new company, and got the same people who bought stock in the old company to buy stock in the new company. The promise was this would really make the company and stock take-off, which would allow them to recover their losses in the first stock deal. To make matters worse they then did it one more time before it all collapsed. Hundreds of thousands of dollars was lost all within the same group of people because they bought the storyline multiple times.

OK, now I know how they do it, how can I protect myself from falling victim to this scam? Do your basic due diligence. Google: the names of the principals of the company, all the companies listed in their press releases to make sure they are real companies, check out the industry they claim they are doing business. Check with the SEC to make sure their stock listing is still current and has not expired; or that there are no sanctions issued against the company. Read their financial report that was provided to the SEC when they initially registered the company. Contact a broker to get their opinion on the company and its press release; as well as to make sure they have not been delisted from the Pink Sheets listings.

This is your money, but be sure you have done your homework before just jumping into something that sounds so good you don't want to pass it up. It doesn't take that long to check things out. It is better to be safe than sorry.

In the next chapters we will identify the type of Internet investment scams called Non-HYIP and HYIP (High Yield Programs). I will give you illustrations of real scams that thousands of people fell victim too, as well as losing millions and millions of dollars. I will explain the truth and the fiction.

The Non-HYIP Scam

First let's restate what a HYIP and a Non-HYIP are. HYIP stands for High Yield Investment Program. A HYIP means the investments supposedly being used for the program to provide you your rate of return are high risk. These investments fall into the category of Commodities Trading, FOREX (Currency) Trading, Oil and Gas Investments, Derivatives, Options Trading, Sports Arbitrage Betting, Gambling, and Arbitrage Trading A Non-HYIP means the risk is supposedly lower, but not far from being high risk. It's the illusion of not being high risk. The types of investments they trade in are: real estate, insurance products, private placement investments, IPO's (Initial Public Offerings), and stock-swaps. Now that we have an understanding of the different types of investments each of these represent, I am going to give an example of each type of program, and dissect it just like I need in the beginning of the book in our Anatomy of a Scam. First let's give an example of one Non-HYIP program called the Reverse Pension Plan.

The premise behind the reverse pension plan is this: there is a Trust, consisting of a group of high net-worth individuals (supposedly Billionaires), who need your personal information so they can purchase a pension plan in your name. This pension plan is a type of a hybrid pension plan and endowment plan rolled into one. To accomplish this task they want you to pay a nominal administration fee of $40. You will submit your personal documents to the trust, and in turn they will issue you a pension policy in the amount of $200,000. But before you are required to pay the premiums for this policy, you will assign the policy to the trust; and the trust is responsible for the premium payments. For you assisting them, they will pay you a lump sum amount of $55,000 (if more than 21 and under 65 at issue, and if under 21 at issue you will receive $110,000). In addition, for helping them reach a specified goal of 100,000 policies, they will pay you a referral fee for each person you have sign-up for the plan of $2,000.

GPP OFFICIAL PLAN DESCRIPTION FROM WEBSITE:

Normal pension plans require the policyholder to turn 65 or 70 years of age before benefits are paid out to the member. That means waiting years, even decades before any financial benefit is derived from the plan whether paid for by a company, the employee or jointly. Additionally, a less favorable point of normal pension savings is the older you are when you enter the program, the more you are required to pay to gain at least reasonable benefits when payout commences.

Based on our vast experience and extensive contacts in the financial world acquired over decades, we have succeeded in creating a very unique plan with a reputable partner. When you are invited to become a member of Global Pension Plan, your only out of pocket cost to register is 30 EUR. This fee covers all of the expenses (administration, processing, maintaining the data base and web sites, handling, banking solution, shipping, etc.) involved to maintain your Global Pension Plan membership. You will not be asked to pay any additional fees or expenses to receive Compensation and/or the Loyalty Program Rewards.

The face value for each member\'s pension plan contract is €200,000. Of this amount 60% or €120,000/75% or €150.000 will be disbursed as follows:

Amount to be distributed for persons aged 27 or younger

Premium for the policy   €16,000
Loyalty Program Rewards (€2,000 x 12 levels) €24,000
Compensation   €110,000
Total amount disbursed   €150,000

Amount to be distributed for persons aged 28 or older

Premium for the policy   €41,000
Loyalty Program Rewards (€2,000 x 12 levels) €24,000
Compensation   €55,000
Total amount disbursed   €120,000

Each of these disbursements is made by the Trust Partner, not the member.(Mortgaging the pension contract is similar to a real estate property mortgage. The contract becomes collateral and is a legally binding agreement provided by a reputable company.)

The item of expenditure most interesting to each member is the one-time Compensation of €55,000 / €110,000 paid to each qualifying member a few months after the 100,000-member quota has been reached. Loyalty Program Rewards will be paid out simultaneously and could be substantial also, depending on effort.

Each contract matures on the 67th birth date of the member. Once the member, named in the contract, has received compensation in the amount of €55,000 / €110,000, they have no further financial interest or liability in the program. The contract premium is also paid in full for the Trust Partner.

Calculations For Members Aged 27 and Younger:

Contract maturity value when member becomes 67 years of age-collateral	€200,000
Percent of contract mortgaged	75%
Cash available for immediate disbursal	€150,000
Contract premium	€16,000
Compensation to member	€110,000
Loyalty Program Rewards €2,000 X 12 levels	€24,000
Total Cash Disbursed When 100,000 Members Under Age 66 Register	€150,000

Calculations For Members Aged 28 and Over:

Contract maturity value when member becomes 67 years of age-collateral	€200,000

Percent of contract mortgaged	60%
Cash available for immediate disbursal	€120,000
Contract premium	€41,000
Compensation to member	€55,000
Loyalty Program Rewards €2,000 X 12 levels	€24,000
Total Cash Disbursed When 100,000 Members Under Age 66 Register	€120,000

Loyalty Program

Active members under the age of 67 who choose to refer new members to Global Pension Plan will receive Compensation and Loyalty Program Rewards. Persons older than 66 years of age on the date of signing the documents do not qualify for Compensation of €55,000; however, they can qualify for the Loyalty Program Rewards! Each member referred by you or by someone else connected to you down 12 levels will earn you a €2,000 Loyalty Program Reward.

You may place as many new members on your first level as you choose. You are not required to work for yourself or the program in general, however, if you choose to do so, full time Administration offers you the support needed to expand the member-base of your TEAM. Our goal is to acquire 100,000 members as quickly as possible so you will find us a very helpful bunch.

As a participant in the Global Pension Plan\'s Loyalty Program you agree to share the unique URL to your personal web site with people you desire to be financially blessed. You are not required to reveal any other personal information. Although we doubt this will ever happen, we want to be clear that any harassment of a non-member by a Global Pension Plan member will result in the forfeiture of all accrued Loyalty Program Rewards from the whole TEAM of that member. In addition, that member will be disqualified from future participation in the

Loyalty Program. This rule will be strictly enforced to prevent the program from gaining a bad reputation and other potential problems. In the event there is a complaint, both individual\'s comments will be evaluated by Administration so as to make a fair decision before any action is taken.

Some food for thought

The following scenario could be yours when you share this program with two people you think could use more money. You direct them to the web site GPP provides for you upon registration and they both decide to register as a member after they have studied the plan. They are as motivated as you are and know two people who they think might be interested in GPP\'s program. They share the business plan with them and those two persons decide to become a member also. When everyone shows the same enthusiasm, the doubling effect continues by members who are on your TEAM and other teams.

When your organization is filled to the 8th level (out of 12 levels), there would be 510 members: (2+4+8+16+32+64+128+256) on your TEAM. For your efforts in sharing with two and helping them share with two who join the program and continuing duplication by every-one you will earn €1,020,000 in Loyalty Program Rewards +€55,000 / €110,000* in Compensation. Remember, there are 4 more levels available to expand your T.E.A.M. (Together Everyone Accomplishes More)! You are not restricted (nor are you required) to find two people to join your TEAM, so use your imagination and build wide. How can this be done? Just by sharing the program with two of your friends and asking them to do the same!

* You must be younger than 67 years of age at the time of payout to qualify for the Compensation.

Miscellaneous Navigational Links

- Disclaimer
- Risk Disclosure
- Privacy Policy

Here is the marketing material they used to get people to sign up for this program: This is exactly as presented, with all typos and misspelled words. Please note there are discrepancies between the original information on the website and their marketing material. This will be addressed in the analysis of the material.

MARKETING MATERIAL:

http://www.globalpensionplan.net

The program we offer for prospective members includes a few exceptional features when compared to any other so called income programs or opportunities.

First of all, we have all the financial resources needed to launch and run an operation this size. Secondly, we have the experience to organize and run an operation with a memberbase of 100,000 at minimum.

We also have extensive contacts in the financial world dating back decades. And last but not least, one of the most important factors in any business with online context is the capable and reliable IT-partner, which we have had from the very beginning of the project working with us turning our vision into reality and making our goals more easily achievable.

Below is a straightforward information of our program called Global Pension Plan. Presentation of this information is not intended to be, nor is it to be construed as, an offer to sell securities, anything pertaining to a security offering, or a solicitation of any offer concerning the information described.

Global Pension Plan is nothing more complicated than a simple pension insurance. However, the program we have established makes it possible for our members to receive the financial benefits in a few months compared to years or decades in case of normal pension insurance. It also removes all the other negative details of the normal pension insurance savings and turns it into a tempting opportunity.

Normally, according to the policy, once the holder of the pension insurance turns 65 or 70, the insurance matures and the benefits will be paid out. This means waiting of years, even decades before benefiting from the financial sacrifices person have made out of the salary months after months, years after years for even 45 years. Also a less favourable point of the normal pension insurance savings is that the later you enter the policy, the more you are required to pay premiums to gain at least reasonable benefits when the policy matures.

Based on our extensive experience and vast contacts in financial world during the last few decades, we have succeeded in establishing a very unique plan around the basic idea of pension insurance with a reputable partner. By becoming a member of Global Pension Plan, You will get the pension insurance for a minimal flat rate of $35 . The fee includes all the expenses (processing, handling, anonymous debit card, shipping etc.) involved into Your Global Pension Plan membership and you will not be asked to pay any additional fees or expenses to receive the Compensation and the Loyalty Program Rewards.

The next step towards the completion of our business plan is that our organization pledge the pension insurance contract of yours for 60% of the face value of $200,000 giving a liquid assets of $120,000 to proceed further (please see the accurate calculations below). Out of this amount will be paid the single premium payment of member's insurance policy, worth $41,000 (the anticipated average premium of 34 years old person).

(Mortgaging the pension insurance contract is similar to property mortgaging when using the property itself as a collateral. The policy is a legally binding agreement given by a reputable insurance company.)

The most tempting item of expenditure from the member's aspect is the one-time Compensation of $55,000 paid out few months after the sign up and the closure of the program from new sign ups. On the very same date of the Compensation payout the Loyalty Program Rewards will also be processed and paid out (please see more details below).

On the very date the insured individual turns 67 and thus the policy matures, the insurance is paid in full for the Trust Partner. At this time the insured individual is not going to receive benefits anymore as he or she has already received the Compensation of $55,000, so there is no need to reflect on the program since you have received the funds.

Calculations:

Pension insurance maturity value 200,000
The percentage of the mortgage 60%
Liquid cash available after the mortgage 120,000
Policy premium 41,000
Compensation 55,000
Loyalty Program Rewards – $2,000 per level X12 levels 24,000
TOTAL 120,000

Loyalty Program

For the active members, who want to bring new members into the Global Pension Plan, we have developed the Loyalty Program which offers tempting rewards, called Loyalty Program Rewards. Even a person older than 66 years, who doesn't qualify for the $55,000 Compensation, may sign up the Loyalty Program and earn the Rewards!

Each new member signing up to your downline down to 12th level, either brought into the program by you or by one of the members in you downline, will earn you $2,000.

You may place as many new members into your first level as you like. We don't want to limit your enthusiams to work for yourself or us. We will also offer you all the support you need while expanding the memberbase of your downline.

As a participant in the Global Pension Plan's Loyalty Program you agree to share your member ID with the new member. You don't have to reveal any other information if you don't want to.

Although we doubt this will ever happen, we want to be clear that any harassment of a non-member person by a Global Pension Plan member will result in the forfeiture of all accrued Loyalty Program Rewards from the whole downline of that member. In addition, that member will be disqualified from future participation in the Loyalty Program. We are extremely strict here to prevent gaining a bad reputation and further problems. In the case of a complaint, both parties will naturally be heard by us to be able to make fair decision before any further actions.

Case study

Let's imagine the following simplified scenario, that by accident you happen to know two persons you want to share this program with and you think would need or want a little more money. You show them our site and they both decide to sign up after they have done their own due diligence. They are as lucky as you are and know two persons as well who they think might be interested in our program.

They share the business plan with them and these two persons decide to sign up as well. Same simple chart continues, it's spread by members who are in your organization. When your organization has grown to the 8th level (out of 12 levels), there are 510 members altogether in your downline and you have earned a reasonable $1,020,000 for your efforts. Plus the $55,000 Compensation of course! And remember, there are still 4 more levels available to expand your downline! Nothing stops your downline growing from here on!

How this can be done? Just by sharing the program with two of your friends and ask them to do the same!

Q&A:

Global Pension Plan Info Pages

GPP is a Trust in Lichtenstein

We want to keep as low profile as possible, not to attract too much publicity and most certainly not to disturb any national bureaucrats with our program.

Q: Is it possible that my application is rejected?

A: Generally, no. Only if you provide false identification information of yourself, there is a slight possibility the insurance company may decide to reject your application.

The insurance company has worked together with our Trust Partner to be able to generate a special insurance policy for our needs. When applying, there won't be questions asked concerning your health conditions or history, living habits, work conditions, hobbies, etc. the Compensations and Loyalty Program Rewards are not paid until the application of the very last member, the 100,000th, has been handled and approved. When the payout happens, there will be a delay of only 20 minutes between the first and last payout. So, practically every member is paid simultaneously and is able to start using the funds via the anonymous debit card.

Q: With the nature of today's financial world, how is Global Pension Plan able to stay clear of the securities and exchange commissions or similar government intrusions worldwide?

A: We are based offshore and online, far away from each and every Big Brother country in the world. We are privacy-minded people and think that nobody should be forced to lose his or her personal privacy for any reason. The securities and exchange commissions, or any other Big Brother government agencies have no jurisdiction whatsoever over our business practices. Furthermore our site and servers are also located outside the USA, EU, Australia, New Zealand etc. and our banking is done in top of the line offshore banking location. Global

Pension Plan has taken steps to insure that our business, and our members' financial future is both safe and secure without the risk to be spoiled by way too jealous governmental bodies.

We also keep as low profile as possible. We don't advertise in newspapers or on TV, we keep our voice down and let the members discreetly market the opportunity to their existing business partners, family members, friends etc. All the advertising done by ourselves is targeted to people already aware of offshore investments and opportunities.

Q: Why does the Trust Partner want to do this business? What is the whole point of it?

A: Our partner is a wealthy offshore trust with long-term objectives. As the anticipated average age of the program members is 34 years, it takes about the same time before the pension insurance policies matures and the benefit of $200,000 is paid to the Trust Partner.

Q: Why don't You reveal the name of the insurance company you cooperate with or the name of the Trust Partner.

A: Because we want to succeed in this business, we need to protect the privacy of all or our partners. This may sound confusing and shady, but please try to take another perspective. If we reveal the name of the insurance company, what would most possibly happen? Hundreds, thousands or even tens of thousands of people would call them to verify the information. That would most probably lead to a huge work load, frustration and delays in the office of the insurance company.

So please let us act as your middle-man taking care of all the contacts and making the program succeed! That's our duty and that's what we are prepared to do.

As we don't identify our partners publicly, we neither identify our members!

Q: What should I tell people if they say: "It is too good to be true"?

A: As mentioned earlier, this program is more or less once in a life-time opportunity. Any interested party should do their own due diligence prior to making a decision for participation. At Global Pension Plan, the prospective members are either familiar with this type of program or have received materials and briefing through an existing member, their sponsor. A question probably rises: "Why should anyone spend the time and effort to promote a bona-fide program that doesn't earn profits during the progress?" The answer is easily found from the difference between the wealthy class and the working class, which is that the wealthy class knows how to make their money work for them even during their sleep, while the working class uses their money to spend on what the wealthy class wants them to spend it on. The way the wealthy class manage to maintain and im-prove their level of wealth is by providing only limited opportunities for the working class, while keeping the privilege opportunities for themselves. This is what you have heard as "The rich getting richer".

Q: How can the policies be mortgaged if they are not paid for yet?

A: This is possible because the premiums haven't been paid for yet. Both the insurance company and one of the mortgaging financial institutions are owned by the same company. Thus the mortgaging institution doesn't have a risk of any kind as they can play by the rules of the house and have control over the monetary issues all the time.

Q: What does the Trust Partner pay in this Program?

A: The Trust Partner pays about $4 - $5 per every new member in addition to the membership fee of $30 EUR out of it's own pocket currently. So please understand the collected membership fees of $3,5M is actually -$450,000 for them. They decided to set the fee to $30 EUR to show some goodwill, but also because $40 would have been too much for most of the people.

Q: What is the "1M For Children" Charity Plan?

A: It is our passionate project to help children of developing countries through our program. The basic idea is to deduct just â,¬10 from the Compensation of each member, which then equals 1M. Each member is, however, free to donate as much into the charity as he/she wants to, there are no limits. The plan will be carried out with an experienced partner to make the funds last as long as possible.

Global Pension Plan is operated by professionals from different walks of life, including accountants, auditors, business and legal consultants with a wealth of experience both locally and worldwide, as well as online.

The Global Pension Plan opportunity has several unique and very lucrative features when compared to other "financial programs" being offered in the world today, including:

- a one-time membership fee of only 30 EUR
- only 100,000 members allowed to join
- €110,000 or €55,000 to you (depending on your age), once membership goal is achieved
- Compensation €110,000 for those 27 or younger
- Compensation €55,000 for those 28 to 66
- anyone 67 or older can promote or buy Plans for their family and earn Loyalty Rewards
- €2,000 Loyalty Rewards Plan for every member you sign up, through 12 levels
- no waiting for retirement to take advantage of this exciting program
- once the 100,000 membership goal is attained, this program will be closed

We at Global Pension Plan have all the financial resources needed to launch and manage an operation this size as well as the experience to organize and maintain an operation with a target of 100,000 members. Additionally, we have extensive contacts in the financial world acquired over decades. All of this expertise makes it possible to offer this time-sensitive, enormously lucrative opportunity to you.

Last, but not least, one of the most important factors in a program of this nature is a capable and reliable IT-partner (computer software developer) which we have. Global Pension Plan draws on the knowledge, experience and resources of a worldwide network to create a uniquely effective and rewarding financial opportunity for You!

Now that you have seen the information provided in the marketing material, the Q&A material, as well as the official information on the website, if you have not seen the warnings this is a scam, let's break it down for you using just this material. After five years of one delaying tactic after another with seven missed payment deadlines, you can imagine all the information that GPP and the promoters of this program have presented to keep the members believing this is real. There is just too much of this information to present. Besides, all you really need to know about this program is contained in the material I have presented. Now let's break it down.

When this plan was first introduced it was limited to only one policy per person registering, and they needed 100,000 members and the program would be closed. This was when it was offered in May 2005. Then in 2007 the admin of GPP advised people they could now purchase more than one policy as they were expanding the number of policies from 100,000 to 350,000; thus an additional 250,000 policies could be bought. GPP also stated the availability of these additional policies would not delay the payment for the first 100,000 policies. When these additional policies were not selling as quickly as they thought, they then began offering the policies at a discount and went as low as $10 per policy. The reason this is important is because in their Q&A they told how much the Trust was paying per policy to offer this benefit. This new policy pricing meant the Trust was paying 75% of the cost per policy. Hopefully just in this explanation there are warning bells, and red lights are flashing telling you this is a scam. I am only going to dissect the most pertinent parts of the plan description.

THE OFFICIAL WEBSITE PLAN DESCRIPTION:

Each scam has about 2%-5% truth to it, and the rest is all fiction. Sadly most people believe the 95% that is fiction as the truth, and the 2%-5% of the truth as the fiction. In this case, the opening paragraph is the only thing they said that is true. Everything after that is all fabricated. But here's the second paragraph:

Based on our vast experience and extensive contacts in the financial world acquired over decades, we have succeeded in creating a very unique plan with a reputable partner. When you are invited to become a member of Global Pension Plan, your only out of pocket cost to register is 30 EUR. This fee covers all of the expenses (administration, processing, maintaining the data base and web sites, handling, banking solution, shipping, etc.) involved to maintain your Global Pension Plan membership. You will not be asked to pay any additional fees or expenses to receive Compensation and/or the Loyalty Program Rewards.

Now do you really believe they can do all of that for just €30? The administration costs alone would be more than €30. Also note they do not reference who their "reputable partner" is, or for that matter who they are.

In the Food for Thought section under Loyalty Program there is this gem:

When everyone shows the same enthusiasm, the doubling effect continues by members who are on your TEAM and other teams. When your organization is filled to the 8th level (out of 12 levels), there would be 510 members (2+4+8+16+32+64+128+256) on your TEAM. For your efforts in sharing with two and helping them share with two who join the program and continuing duplication by everyone you will earn €1,020,000 in **Loyalty Program Rewards** +€55,000 / €110,000 in **Compensation**.

This loyalty bonus will come into play later when we break all this down financially to see if this is even remotely possible. Remember, if someone has referrals 12 levels down, his or her loyalty bonus reward is €1,020,000, but if each 12 does the same and each goes down 12 levels, your loyalty bonus reward payment would be €16, 392,000.

Now let's dissect the marketing material:

MARKETING MATERIAL:

The first three paragraphs are nothing more than trying to convince you the people behind this program are capable of administering, and bringing this program to a successful payout. The fact they emphasized their IT Partner and how important this relationship is to their success will come back and bite them later. About half-way through this programs run, their system was hacked, the database was hacked, the system was down due to a DDOS attack, and anyone could access anyone's back office. So much for their claim about a capable and reliable IT Partner when presenting this program initially.

They claim this reverse pension plan is a "simple pension plan" that makes it possible for our members to receive the financial benefits in a few months compared to years or decades as in a normal pension insurance plan. Yet when it people started exposing this as a scam on the Internet investment forums, suddenly it became a complicated hybrid pension plan, and of course, those of us who were not in the program were not entitled to know how it worked.

Based on our extensive experience and vast contacts in financial world during the last few decades, we have succeeded in establishing a very unique plan around the basic idea of pension insurance with a reputable partner. By becoming a member of Global Pension Plan, You will get the pension insurance for a minimal flat rate of $35 . The fee includes all the expenses (processing, handling, anonymous debit card, shipping etc.) involved into Your Global Pension Plan membership and you will not be asked to pay any additional fees or expenses to receive the Compensation and the Loyalty Program Rewards.

Well, as mentioned in the information setting up this program, other fees were requested when they offered the extra policies for each person, and then later when they asked people to send in their personal information for processing. Seems those hackers, the great and reliable IT Partner could not prevent, sent out E-mails to the membership asking for fees to be paid for courier delivery of their checks supposedly representing their payment. Another hacker also sent out an E-mail to the membership telling them they had to purchase a debit card, and had three different types of cards from which to choose, and of course, requiring additional fees to be paid. In all fairness, the people who ran this scam did not request these fees, but they were believed to have been done by members of GPP who wanted to recoup their losses because they realized they had been scammed. Still, the people behind GPP allowed this to happen with having no security whatsoever on their website and the membership database.

They then proceeded to give an illustration of how the money would be paid to the members from the borrowing 60% of the face value of the policy of $200,000. They borrowed 60% of the face value which made a loan of $120,000. Of this, $55,000 was paid to the member, $41,000 was for premium payment, and the balance of $24,000 was the loyalty bonus for having referred 12 people into the program.

From looking at these numbers, all seems to be in order. But there are major flaws in their mathematical calculations. First they do not allow for the people who obtain referrals 12 levels down that would represent referral fees of $1,020,000 as illustrated from the OFFICIAL PLAN DESCRIPTION. But it is even worse than that. If you referred two people and each of them referred just two people, and everyone 12 levels deep did the same, your total loyalty bonus reward payment would be a whopping $16, 392,000.

Just using these numbers, and only allowing 100,000 people to be paid without the loyalty program, the total CASH a lending institution would be lending is $12 Billion. Now if they sold all the additional 250,000 policies, this payment would now balloon to $70 Billion. This factor alone proves this is a scam. The top 100 lending institutions or banks in the world could not pay out in CASH this much money at one time. When you add in there is no insurance company in the world who could underwrite and issue this many policies, is another nail in the coffin of this being a real program.

But the statements that were major red flag warnings that I have underlined and bolded were these from the Q & A section where they said:

To stay alive, we must keep a low profile and stay together. We have met difficulties, like SPAM and DDoS attacks, but all of them have been beaten successfully! **It's normal to experience attacks from naysayers who want to destroy something extraordinary.** But because of a professional online presence plan, we are still available for the general public.

The Trust Partner pays about $4 - $5 per every new member in addition to the membership fee of $30 EUR out of it's own pocket currently. **So please understand the collected membership fees of $3,5M is actually -$450,000 for them. They decided to set the fee to $30 EUR to show some goodwill, but also because $40 would have been too much for most of the people.**

We are based offshore and online, far away from each and every Big Brother country in the world. We are privacy-minded people and think that nobody should be forced to lose his or her personal privacy for any reason. The securities and exchange commissions, or any other Big Brother government agencies have no jurisdiction whatsoever over our business practices. Furthermore our site and servers are also located outside the USA, EU, Australia, New Zealand etc. and our banking is done in top of the line offshore banking location. **Global Pension Plan has taken steps to insure that our business, and our members' financial future is both safe and secure without the risk to be spoiled by way too jealous governmental bodies.**

We also keep as low profile as possible. We don't advertise in newspapers or on TV, we keep our voice down and let the members discreetly market the opportunity to their existing business partners, family members, friends etc. All the advertising done by ourselves is targeted to people already aware of offshore investments and opportunities.

Now if what I have bolded and underlined did not raise any issues in your mind, then you could be one of the more than 350,000 people who joined this program that did not give these issues one-minute of thought. They have told you they are a scam just with the information I have bolded and underlined. But in case you were still wondering, here are more reasons why this is a scam:

- First, you cannot borrow against the face amount of $200,000 because the policy has no value. It only has value as you pay the premiums. Think of it this way. Take a jar and each month you put $100 into the jar. The jar represents the pension policy and the $100 represents the monthly premium. Until you put money into the jar, there is no cash value of the pension policy. Now they used an average premium of $41,000 in their example from above. So let's put $41,000 into the jar. What is the most you can draw out of the jar? Of course $41,000. But they said they would pay you $55,000 (if more than 21 and under 65), plus $24,000 for your referrals. So where does the money that exceeds $41,000 come from? Then consider the people under 21 that are promised $110,000 and the $24,000 in referral fees. Also where does the $1,020,000 or the $16, 392,000 Loyalty Bonus come from if you qualified for it? Understand how this is impossible now?

- Second a $200,000 pension plan has considerable first year costs associated with the purchase of the policy, none of which are covered in the example they gave as this being real. Use the example from above, and you see this becomes even more impossible to do.
- Third, not everyone would qualify for a $200,000 pension policy, as it is based on age, your income, projected income, and your ability to pay the premiums.
- Fourth, you would also be required to pass a health test, which is not required by them for you to participate in this program. For these reasons alone, is why these policies are a scam.
- Fifth, you do not know the name of the Trust partners;
- Sixth, you do not know the name of the company behind this;
- Seventh, you do not know the name of the insurance company; and
- Eight, you don't know the name of the bank or lending institution who will loan the money.

Not only do you not know their names, you do not have an address, phone number, or contact information of any kind for any of these entities. All you know is the first name of the admin, but only a first name. The admin has a free E-mail account such as Stella@gmail.com. So you cannot verify any of the information is true, or do any type of real due diligence.

I hope that you now understand how to spot the salient points from the Q&A as well as the Marketing Material that demonstrate this is a scam without my having to point each and every one of them out to you. I am confident you get it.

SO LET'S RECAP:

Mathematically this is impossible to be done;

It is impossible for this many policies to be underwritten and issued by one insurance company, as they claim in their marketing material;

It is a myth that being registered offshore prevents the U.S. regulatory agencies from extraditing you and bringing charges against you.

The fact they explicitly tell you they are illegal by declaring they have to stay below the radar of governmental agencies worldwide.

They wanted to keep a low profile, but they are all over the Internet kind of defeats this purpose don't you think?

There is no address, phone number or names of the people in this Trust.

There is no name, address, phone number for the insurance company.

There is no name, address, phone number for the lending institution.

The only contact information you have to reach them is an E-mail address of stella@gmail.com. That's it. Real professional don't you think?

Yes, I remember them saying they had to keep this information private as they valued privacy; but that was all smoke and mirrors so they could not be reported to the authorities. Hard to report someone when you don't know who they are or where they are located. Offering this program on the Internet is not exactly "keeping a low profile" as they claimed.

Now let's examine the HYIP programs, and see how they are similar to the Non-HYIP as far as red flag warnings, but differ in types of investments. These are the programs that are the most prevalent of the Internet investment scams. While the types of investments are different, the results are the same. They are scams and will separate you from your money.

The HYIP Scam

The most prevalent of the Internet investment scams are the High Yield Investment Programs-HYIP. They also represent over 75% of the money stolen on the Internet today. Like their Non-HYIP counterpart, many register offshore and think because they are, they are not subject to the U.S. regulatory agencies or compliance with the U.S. Securities Laws. Nothing could be further from the truth, but when you have unsophisticated investors checking out these programs, they believe what they are told; and want to participate due to the high rate of return these programs promise. The other lure to these programs is the promise that their "Principal is Guaranteed." Nothing could be further from the truth. To select which HYIP program I wanted to illustrate and expose was a hard decision, because there are so many good ones to choose from. This dilemma is further compounded by whether to choose a FOREX, Sports Arbitrage Betting, Commodities, or one that claimed to be loan-sharking as their source of revenue for their investment program. No I am not kidding about the loan sharking program, but they called it being "financial mercenaries." Either way the people joining this program weren't bothered how they earned on their investment, just that they did. Of course in all fairness this was not prominently displayed on the website, nor was it mentioned in any of the promotions on the forums about the program; but still it was there for all to see if they looked. So I have decided to show a FOREX and the one that claimed they were being financial mercenaries, but in reality was loan sharking. Here is the information exactly from pages on their website:

WHITE FUND

COMPANY PROFILE

Assets Management Services Powered By Mechanical Trading Systems:

White Fund is an online managed forex fund. Our unique multi-strategy approach allows us to achieve aggressive growth of assets over a long-term investment horizon while preserving invested capital through limited drawdowns. We have been providing private assets management services to high net worth individuals since the beginning of 2003, and in 2010 we opened White Fund Online to general public. Our track record is long and distinguished, and our commitment to excellence is reflected in our performance.

Trading Strategy

White Fund uses four proprietary trading systems. Our trading strategy is 90% systematic with a 10% discretionary component. We manage investors' funds using one or several trading systems depending on the investment plan: WF Mercury alone in Short-term portfolio, WF Mercury, WF Dynamic and WF CS in Medium-term, and WF Mercury, WF Dynamic, WF CS and WF Stats combined in the Long-term portfolio.

OUR INVESTMENT PROGRAMS:

Short-Term Portfolio

- 1.5% Daily Profit, paid on trading days
  $20 Minimum Investment, $2,000
  Maximum 30 trading days investment period
  Systems traded: WF Mercury
  Principal return after maturity

Medium-Term Portfolio

- 1.9% Daily Profit, paid on trading days
  $100 Minimum Investment, $10,000 Maximum
  60 trading days investment period
  Systems traded: WF Mercury, WF Dynamic, WF CS
  Principal return after maturity

Long-Term Portfolio

- 2.2% Daily Profit, paid on trading days
  $1,000 Minimum Investment, $50,000 Maximum

180 trading days Investment period
Systems traded: WF Mercury, WF Dynamic, WF CS, WF
Stats
Principal return after maturity

Affiliate Program

5% Referer Commissions

Special Bonus Offer

9%   **DEPOSIT**   **BONUS!**
Make a new deposit $1,000 - $2,000 to any Investment Portfolio
through the end of June and receive a 9% Bonus to your Account
Balance!

11%   **DEPOSIT**   **BONUS!**
Make a new deposit over $2,000 to any Investment Portfolio through
the end of June and receive a 11% Bonus to your Account Balance!

OUR MANAGEMENT TEAM:

John Williams, Co-Founder and President

John Williams was the one who created White Fund in 2002. Mr.
Williams has been in the trading business for almost 40 years, having
gotten started back in 1971. He began his career at Bank of America
North Carolina, and then Goldman Sachs where he served as a Trader
and then a Senior Trader for 19 years. Then he joined Dunn Capital
Management, one of the most successful Commodity Trading Advisor
(CTA) of all times. In late 2002 John Williams in cooperation with
Matthew Goldstein started an offshore White Fund to provide private
assets management services for high net worths individuals. Mr.
Williams' educational background includes MBA degree from the
University of Chicago and a Bachelor of Science degree in both
Finance and Economics from the University of North Carolina. John
enjoys traveling with his wife, spending time with his family, and
playing various sports such as golf, basketball, and soccer.

Matthew Goldstein, Co-Founder and Vice President, Technology

Mr. Goldstein is responsible for the creation of all technical aspects of the program's analytical model development and the overall portfolio's ongoing proficiency. He established the proprietary testing trading platform which forms the basis for the White Fund investment process, focusing on its flexibility and robustness. Matthew has been developing and trading quantitative strategies for more than 10 years, working at several big Wall Street firms such as Goldman Sachs and Bear Stearns, before launching White Fund in 2002 with John Williams. Mr. Goldstein holds a MS degree in Mathematics and Computer Science from the University of North Carolina. Mr. Goldstein spends his free time with his wife and his 3 sons. They enjoy sports, especially basketball & hockey, snowboarding and skiing.

Susan McBrite, Vice President, Finance

She joined White Fund with deep experience in finance and accounting roles as a Corporate Controller and CFO. Susan has a broad base of experience in financial operations and controls, human resources, risk management, and tax compliance. Mrs. McBrite is a Certified Public Accountant and earned her Master of Professional Accounting in Tax/Finance from the University of Washington.

Anne Lister, Vice President, Investor Relations

Anne joined White Fund team in early 2009, bringing with her 7 years of experience in financial services, the majority of this time focused on consumer banking and insurance products. Prior to her appointment Anne held a number of management positions in HSBC San Antonio. Mrs. Lester holds a BS degree in Business Administration by the University of Texas in 2001.

Experience is the key to success. Co-Founders of White Fund have over 50 years combined experience as investment bankers and fund managers.

Frequently Asked Questions

General Questions:

Is White Fund a HYIP?

White Fund is an investment program. Almost all so-called HYIPs are pyramid or Ponzi schemes where profits of previous investors are paid with the money invested by new-comers. Such schemes are destined to collapse because there are little or no underlying earnings from the money received by the promoter.

Contrary to this, we are real traders and we trade investors' funds on foreign exchange markets using our proven, robust trading systems.

Can I lose money?

We can guarantee that our members' money are safe. We are not here to lose, and since its inception in 2002 White Fund has produced excellent returns. Although we cannot provide 100% risk free profits, our trading systems are so robust, that for seven years as we trade investors' money White Fund had only three negative months! So we're sure that unless something extraordinary like third world war happens, we will continue making money for our clients. And our reserve fund provides extra guarantee of stable daily payments to program participants.

What are you going to do with my money after I invest it?

After receiving your funds we will deliver it to our Forex trading account so your investment start making profit for you.

Why do you have fixed rates of return and not profit sharing?

We offer fixed rates as we believe that fixed profit rate gives investors more confidence in investment and stability of payouts regardless of current market conditions. The Fund experiences drawdowns from time to time, but we go through them paying out investors from our stabilization fund.

Which e-currencies do you accept?

We accept Liberty Reserve and Perfect Money. They were chosen due to their large market share and independence from jurisdiction of any state.

Do you pay profits directly into my e-currencies account?

Your profits will be credited to your White Fund account under "Account Balance". This balance can further be reinvested or withdrawn at any time. We do not pay interests directly into your e-currencies account for security reasons. It is much safer to credit interest to your Account Balance so that you could then request a withdrawal into your e-currencies. This way we can check and process every withdrawal request manually.

Do you pay on calendar or trading days?

We pay profits on trading days Monday through Friday, except for public holidays when markets are closed.

What if I forgot my User ID or password?

Please use this Username or Password Recovery page and follow the instructions on that page.

How can I change my e-currencies account numbers?

You cannot change an e-currency account number once you provided it for security reasons.

May I open several accounts in your program?

You are not prohibited from having several accounts with us, funded by various payment methods, i.e. one account with Liberty Reserve deposit and another one with Perfect Money deposit. In addition, your accounts from the same IP cannot be referrals of each other, and if we find a member using this practice all referral commissions will be deducted and cheating accounts are subject for 30% deposit charge for investigation purposes.

Can my relative of friend make a deposit to White Fund using the same computer or IP address?

Yes, but these accounts cannot be referrals of each other, and have to use various payment methods, i.e. one account funded by Liberty Reserve and another one by Perfect Money. If we find you generating self-referral commissions these commissions will be deducted and cheating accounts are subject for 30% deposit charge for investigation purposes.

DEPOSIT

How can I deposit funds into my White Fund account?

Log into your White Fund account, click on the 'Make a Deposit' link and follow instructions on that page to deposit funds. Deposits are automated so you see funds in your White Fund account instantly.

Do you provide a wire transfer option?

We decided to accept deposits from e-currencies only. If you prefer wire transfer there's an easy solution: you may wire funds directly into your Perfect Money e-currency account and then invest using Perfect Money by just a mouse click. Click on the "Deposit" link within your Perfect Money members area and choose "Bank Wire", fill in the form and you will receive wire transfer instructions. Additionally you may use any of the official Liberty Reserve exchangers or Perfect Money exchangers to fund your electronic currency account and then invest using e-currency. We recommend using GoldExPay as the most respectful one.

Can I make a deposit via Paypal or another e-currency?

Unfortunately we do not accept deposits via PayPal or other e-currencies except Liberty Reserve and Perfect Money. But you can easily transfer the funds you have in your PayPal account into e-currencies we accept. To do this you need to use an exchanger.

How can I invest by Credit Card?

You may use the following exchange providers to fund e-currencies by Credit Card: CentreGold.ca and ElectrumX.com

What are the deposit limits?

The minimum investment amount is $20. We wanted to make it possible for you to evaluate and see the benefits of investing with White Fund without having to raise substantial investment capital, that's why we have set the minimum deposit requirement to only $20. The maximum limitation depends on the duration of the program. For the Long-Term Program the limit is $50,000. If you would like to invest more please contact us.

Can I make an additional deposit to my White Fund account once it has been opened?

Yes, you can but all deposits have their own locking periods and are handled separately.

Do you provide compounding?

No automatic compounding option - you can reinvest from your account balance manually.

I have funds in my account balance, but I do not want to withdraw them into my e-currencies account, can I add them to my deposit so that they continue earning interest for me?

Yes, to make a deposit from your White Fund account balance simply login into your members account, click on the 'Make a Deposit' link and select the 'Deposit from Account Balance' radio button.

How often can I make deposits into my account?

You can make deposits into your account as often as you want. There are no restrictions in this regard.

WITHDRAWAL

How can I withdraw my money?

Please enter 'Withdraw Money' menu and follow the instructions provided on this page. You can withdraw the funds into your e-currency account or re-invest it back without any fees.

Is withdrawal process automated?

No, for security purposes withdrawal process is not automated.

How long does it take for my withdrawal to be processed?

All withdrawal requests are processed manually after being checked and approved by our managers. Normally withdrawals are processed within 12 hours.

Is the initial investment (principal) returned to me at the end of the investment term?

Yes, your principal will be returned at the end of the investment plan period, and you can withdraw funds from your account principal afterwards.

Can I withdraw my deposit before maturity?

The interest rates we offer on investments are based on the expectation that the funds will be with us for the full term. Therefore there is a 30% fee upon premature deposit cancellation.

Can I withdraw funds to a different e-currency system?

No, you can only request a withdrawal to the e-currency you deposited with.

What are the minimum and maximum amounts that I can withdraw?

The minimum withdrawal is $0.01. There is no maximum withdrawal amount.

Is there a withdrawal fee?

No, we do not have any fees involved with our withdrawals.

How often can I request a withdrawal?

Members are allowed to request a withdrawal anytime.

REFERRAL

How much affiliate commission do you pay?

We pay 5% commission from any investment made by your referred person. It will be added to your Account Balance immediately after your referral's deposit.

Do I need to invest myself in order to participate in your affiliate program?

No, you do not have to invest yourself. You only need to open an account with us.

How do I refer other people to your program and earn referral commission?

You need to provide them with your personal referral link which can be found in 'Account Overview' area in your account. You can advertise this link anywhere on the web (forums, chats, advertising, your own site, mail lists etc).

Can I use SPAM to promote White Fund?

No, spam is strictly prohibited. We do not tolerate SPAM in any of its forms. Any user caught spamming will lose his/her account immediately.

How do you pay referral commission?

Referral commission is added to your Account Balance. Referral commission is paid via the same e-currency type (Liberty Reserve, Perfect Money etc) as the one through which the deposit has been made.

How can I withdraw referral commission from my Withdrawable Balance?

To do this you need to log into your White Fund account, access 'Withdraw Money' area and enter the amount you would like to withdraw.

Why I have not received a referral commission from a person I referred to you?

The most probable reasons are:

- Your referral has opened an account with us, but has not yet made a deposit. Please note that we pay referral commission only after your referral has made a deposit.

- You are not listed as referrer in your referral's account profile. Please ask him/her to contact us about this matter and we will set you as his/her Referrer manually.

SECURITY

What can I do to protect my account password?

Several tips on how to avoid compromising your account password:

- Use a unique account password you have never used with other accounts before.

- Use a non-sense combination of characters and numbers

- Store your password in a safe place, preferably on a removable disk or other storage.

- Avoid copying and pasting your password, try entering it manually. Use a graphical on-screen keyboard when possible to protect against malicious key-logger programs.

I have received an email from you that contains an attachment. Is it safe to open it?

No, never open such attachments! We have never and never will send any emails containing attachments. Such emails are sent by hackers trying to get your account password and other data.

How secure is your website?

We take online investment security very seriously. All transactions are secured by a 1024 bit industry Standard SSL Certificate. SSL creates an encrypted link between our web server and your web browser to ensure that all data transmitted remains private and secure, you can find the page is protected if the URL displayed in the address bar begins with https:// Your password is stored on our server in an encrypted format, which even we cannot decrypt. We guarantee that every transaction you make with White Fund is completely safe.

Will you disclose my personal or investment information?

Your privacy is our business. We will never sell, rent or give away any information provided by you. White Fund will use the information you provide only to verify your identity, and may later on use the information you submit to notify you about WhiteFund.com products and services that you may find useful. Please refer to Privacy Policy for more information.

I still haven't seen here an answer to my question. What should I do?

Please contact us, the support team will be glad to help you at any time.

I am only going to address the program, the bios of the management team, and the three answers of the Q & A, since they are the major areas of importance. By now you should be capable of identifying the red flag warnings from the remainder of the Q&A section. I did remove a few of the Q&A comments as they were not relevant for discussion.

For a company that is supposed to have such a distinguished management team and knowledge of the FOREX market, one would think they would know it is not forex, but FOREX when discussing this trading platform. I know it sounds trivial, but sometimes the devil is in the details. Nowhere on their website do they give an address for their headquarters or where they are located. They also do not tell you where they are registered and licensed to do FOREX trading, which is required by law. Let's further analyze their opening paragraph:

White Fund is an online managed forex fund. Our unique multi-strategy approach allows us to achieve aggressive growth of assets over a long-term investment horizon while preserving invested capital through limited drawdowns. We have been providing private assets management services to high net worth individuals since the beginning of 2003, and in 2010 we opened White Fund Online to general public. Our track record is long and distinguished, and our commitment to excellence is reflected in our performance.

Can anyone tell me what they really said here? They are merely words trying to impress, but says absolutely nothing about the company. They do not mention any clients, and do not provide any information that supports and proves their "long and distinguished track record," or their "excellent performance." Next they discuss their trading strategy:

White Fund uses four proprietary trading systems. Our trading strategy is 90% systematic with a 10% discretionary component. We manage investors' funds using one or several trading systems depending on the investment plan: WF Mercury alone in Short-term portfolio, WF Mercury, WF Dynamic and WF CS in Medium-term, and WF Mercury, WF Dynamic, WF CS and WF Stats combined in the Long-term portfolio.

Short-Term Portfolio

- 1.5% Daily Profit, paid on trading days

$20 Minimum Investment, $2,000 Maximum

- 30 trading days investment period
- Systems traded: WF Mercury
- Principal return after maturity

Medium-Term Portfolio

- 1.9% Daily Profit, paid on trading days
- $100 Minimum Investment, $10,000 Maximum 60 trading days investment period
- Systems traded: WF Mercury, WF Dynamic, WF CS
- Principal return after maturity

Long-Term Portfolio

- 2.2% Daily Profit, paid on trading days
- $1,000 Minimum Investment, $50,000 Maximum
- 180 trading days Investment period
- Systems traded: WF Mercury, WF Dynamic, WF CS, WF Stats
- Principal return after maturity

Again words to impress but they say absolutely nothing that makes any sense. What is a systematic trading strategy and a discretionary component trading strategy? The only thing people who joined this knew is how much return they were supposed to get on their investment. After that they stopped reading, even though they had no clue what they had been told.

Next they provided bios for the principals of the firm. On the website they had these nice pictures of each principal, and a group picture of them in an office setting. All to impress, but were all photo-shopped. Not really them. Also all their bios were fake. I know because I checked each one of them out. I contacted the universities where they claimed to have received their degree, and the employers where they said they were employed before they formed White Fund. No degree as claimed from the schools they claimed to have attended, and no surprise but also no work history at any of the companies claimed.

But the telling signs this was a Pozni was the first two questions they addressed in their Q&A:

Is White Fund a HYIP?

White Fund is an investment program. Almost all so-called HYIPs are pyramid or Ponzi schemes where profits of previous investors are paid with the money invested by new-comers. Such schemes are destined to collapse because there are little or no underlying earnings from the money received by the promoter. Contrary to this, we are real traders and we trade investors' funds on foreign exchange markets using our proven, robust trading systems.

Can I lose money?

We can guarantee that our members' money are safe. We are not here to lose, and since its inception in 2002 White Fund has produced excellent returns. Although we cannot provide 100% risk free profits, our trading systems are so robust, that for seven years as we trade investors' money White Fund had only three negative months! So we're sure that unless something extraordinary like third world war happens, we will continue making money for our clients. And our reserve fund provides extra guarantee of stable daily payments to program participants.

Notice that they never answered either question with a direct answer. They skirted all around it making you think they had, but they avoided an answer. When an investment program has to tell you they are not a Ponzi or a pyramid, they are a Ponzi and a pyramid scheme. This is a major red flag warning, and don't forget it. No reputable company would even raise the issue, as it would cast doubt on their legitimacy immediately.

Notice in the second question they also don't answer it, but claim their client money is safe. They never bother to explain how this is true, but you are just supposed to take their word for it. To further convince you your money is safe they then try to tell you that in seven years they have only had three losing months. Sure sounds like what Bernie Madoff claimed too, and we know what happened to his program. Well the same thing happened here.

And of course, we have the mandatory referral commissions you earn when you get others to join the program. All Ponzi/Scams have this element in their program, and the reason why they expand so quickly.

Do I need to invest myself in order to participate in your affiliate program?

No, you do not have to invest yourself. You only need to open an account with us.

Now stop and think about this answer for a moment. You do not have to invest with them, but they will still pay you a referral fee for getting others to join and invest with them. Name me a brokerage firm, or broker, that will pay you a referral fee if you are not a client? What friend would invest in a program that you were not invested in to begin with? If it was that great of an investment, they would want to know why you haven't invested.

On the financial forums where these programs get traction and they get people to join their programs, I exposed White Fund's management teams bios were fake, and their entire program was a Ponzi. Of course the admin of White Fund posted I didn't know what I was talking about, that I had to be the admin of another program trying to discredit them so they would join my program, and that he personally knew the management team and they were real. Within 48 hours of my exposing White Fund on the financial forums, their website disappeared, and they ran with the money. Leaving the members high and dry losing all they had invested in this Ponzi. So much for their disclaimer in the first question of their Q&A they were not a Ponzi or pyramid scheme.

Now for one of my all-time favorite scams in the past year was a program called PTVPartner. This program appeared in late August of 09 and made numerous claims. To provide all the information contained on their website would be too lengthy, so I am only going to post the most relevant pages. They will demonstrate the points I want to make regarding this program. But one thing their web pages did not cover was a recorded interview with their admin, Garrett Rainier, in which he extolled the amazing discovery they had made of a large silica mine. A mine that not only contained silica, but also: gold, copper, zinc, palladium, platinum, quartzite, geothermal, and a large forest. I kept waiting for them to say they found diamonds, rubies and sapphires at this mine too, since they had found about everything else. The only problem is they could not disclose the location of this mine to the members. Yet they had geologists from all over the world there taking core samples. He claimed this mine had the purest silica anywhere in the world with purity up to 97.99%. This mine was 10 miles long, 2.5 miles wide and 3'-5' deep. The mine was estimated to be 200 billion tons of silica and 8,000 million ounces of gold. Now what Garrett failed to do was a little research, for if he had he would have discovered there were silica mines right here in the USA that had silica that is 99.5% pure. In fact every time you walk on a beach, you are walking on silica. So much for story of the silica mine being true. This alone proved this was a Ponzi. But the real interesting story they told was their being financial mercenaries. Here is the selected content from their website as presented:

PTVPARTNER

The definition of PT: **"What is a PT?"**

PT - means whatever positive concept you can imagine. For example: Perpetual Traveler; Permanent Tourist; Prior Taxpayer; Positive Thinker; Privacy Tactician - and any other positive label you can think of that spells "PT"!

More recently, this personal secession strategy has become known as being an **Internationalist**.

The basic concept is as follows: In order to reduce the effective tyranny of any one jurisdiction over your life - you need to spread your practical life over multiple jurisdictions. You could say it's a strategy for **"hedging your bets"** in life. And just as investment advisors suggest you diversify your investments, so the PT strategy suggests you diversify and **'Free your Life'."**

Who and Why are PTVPartner.com?

Perpetual Traveler Venture (PTV) Partners is the online version of our PT Venture Group. PT Venture Group is an affiliation of some 120 plus PT Associates who began banding together in the late 1970's as friends, acquaintances and eventually business partners.

When the PT lifestyle was originally conceived and promoted, it was designed for those with the financial means to make it work. You either needed to be financially independent, with a private source of income, or have the type of occupation that allowed you to live and work anywhere. The opportunities, afforded a PT, from countries around the world, can be unbelievably lucrative. In many cases the ability to take full advantage of such opportunities is limited to the PT or Sovereign individual.

However, since the advent of the Internet, the possibility of working internationally is now a reality for practically anyone. As experienced PT's we have taken advantage of opportunities afforded a select few, but now we are offering some of those opportunities to you.

PTVGroup Niche

PTVGroup has developed into an International Venture Capitalization Partnership with more than

$200 Million Personally Participated And Billions Amassed Via Private Placement Associates.

Formalized in 1983, the firm has grown to include holdings all across the globe.

From the start, PTVGroup has raised private funds to invest in individuals, governments and communities that are under-served by traditional sources of risk capital. PTVGroup has built a strong and successful track record of public and private partnerships with many varied and diverse economic development organizations, facilitating the flow of billions of dollars of investment capital into these structures.

PTVGroup provides equity and debt capital, along with value-added counsel and other support, to operating businesses that have a high probability for excellent investor returns as well as significant community impact. Our Group uses this dual bottom line to measure its success.

* Our investment profile also spans venture capital, expansion, management buyouts, secondary stock, acquisitions, spinout and recapitalization financings.

* PTVGroup specializes in financial technology, pharmaceutical business solutions, communications, business services and application software.

* Beyond capital, PTVGroup brings considerable value-added services to our portfolio companies. We collaborate with entrepreneurs, service providers, financing sources and acquirers.

Realize it's downright STUPID to invest in dividend-paying stocks....when according to the Financial Times, and we quote "investors are facing the worst year for dividend cuts sine 1918..."

Understand the INSANITY of investing in Pozni Schemes like most Forex, HYIP, Autosurf or PTC opportunities..

Be shown how you can turn a small portfolio into a REAL, 4, 5 or even 6-figure monthly "Dividend" that comes in like clock-work.

There is no substitute. Without funding, no major company could expand. They could not pay their employees, afford to market, seek new accounts, invest in research and development or even accomplish the most basic tasks. Activities would grind to a halt. And as a result of the Current Economic Crises, funding has become more of a necessity than at any other time since the Great Depression... Companies are struggling, going out of business one after another, banks can no longer afford to lend... this means numerous entities worldwide are willing to pay a Premium for access to "expansion" money - they simply need money to grow...

...to stay alive.

That's how we began. In 1975 several of our earliest members had become multi-millionaires. The underground market of lending had grown like wildfire. Private corporate financiers had become among the world's richest middlemen. They ...

Discovered A Way To Collect Abnormally High Returns...

By Providing The Critical Funding Companies Needed!

But here's the beauty! The type of funding provided by these private corporate financiers, these renegade billionaires and associates like the PTVGroup, could not be regulated. After all, 98% of this $5.8 trillion dollar market is hidden from the public. According to the USA Today, "This is a dark and massive corner of the financial markets!"

Nonetheless, it simply means, charging companies 5... 10... 15... even 20 times as much as a bank could - is 100% legal.

Could You Imagine Paying 30, 40 or even 50% Interest On Your Mortgage?

But that's the reality these businesses face. Why? Simply because they have no other choice -- pay it, or go dead. These are the options. Today, like in the 1980's banks and the federal government are up to their ears in red - they can't afford to lend. Even more exciting is the fact, We've located a special segment of companies, although not ready yet, will be offering upwards of 250% monthly return starting in the next few months. And yes, that's a monthly return.

So, Private Financiers, take full advantage. We've been called Financial Mercenaries.

Through Intense Lobbying (For More Than 30 Years) The King-Pins of this Opportunity Have Successfully Protected Our Monopoly From The General Public... And...

To this day, they're still not regulated by any Government, Congress or any other Elected Office.

Now, You Can Invest Alongside Billionaires...

Even If All You Have Is A Few Bucks!

That's right. You see, in the early summer of '08, several of our major players in this market, all got together and changed the rules - it was decided we would make it possible for small investors to in essence piggy-back on our program.

Look. This isn't rocket science. In a nutshell, it's this simple:

Companies need funding... we have money to invest... we give it to them... and in return... they pay Huge Returns.

Yes, if a bank charged this kind of interest, it would be <u>ILLEGAL</u>.

Even more impressive is the fact that we lock these returns in up front. No worrying, wondering, or losing sleep at night trying to predict the fate of the stock market. Is this the bottom? Is that the bottom? Frankly, who the hell knows?

"This Is A REAL, Private Placement Funding, Venture Capitalization Participation Opportunity! ...And Your Principal Is Guaranteed!!!"

"Principle Guarantee — We have dedicated several long term and stable private programs to secure (Guarantee) your front-end deposits until you are in profit. Once your profit exceeds your participation then your account is withdrawn from the security pool. If you re-deposit 'New' funds, in excess of your realized profits, these funds ARE covered by the security pool."

<u>"Q. Are you a registered trading or investment company?</u>

A. As PTVPartner.com no. We are a group of Sovereign Individuals, Internationalists or PT's following the PT lifestyle in both our personal and business lives. While we hold, own, control, trade, move, build, disassemble, manipulate and construct registered and accredited business all over the globe, we choose not to disclose our private information as to not compromise our business relationships. To most, PT is unique. To some perhaps even over the top. Associating our affiliations with our PT status offline could cause unnecessary complications. Those here that feel ill-at-ease regarding our PT status or our lack of transparency should do their own due diligence to establish a comfort level adequate to indulge or refrain from participation."

As I said there's more, but these are the most important parts of their program from their website. By now you should be able to identify some of the red flag warnings, and understand 99% of everything they said was pure make believe. They also made a claim that the PTV Partners had $1 Billion Dollars they were going to be investing into these companies that had no other place to go but to them for cash. Did you also catch where they said your principal was 'Guaranteed?" Did you catch their claim they are financial mercenaries? Here it is: So, Private Financiers, take full advantage. We've been called Financial Mercenaries. Companies need funding... we have money to invest... we give it to them... and in return... they pay Huge Returns. Yes, if a bank charged this kind of interest, it would be ILLEGAL. Nonetheless, it simply means, charging companies 5... 10... 15... even 20 times as much as a bank could - is 100% legal. Sounds like loan sharking to me, how about you?

I began exposing them as a Ponzi scheme back in September of 09. The admin, Garrett Rainier, had done an interview with an online financial blog where he introduced his program, then was immediately introduced on all the financial investment forums where all these Ponzi's get traction. In this interview he went to great lengths to tell how PTVPartners had made sure their system was secure and safe for the members. They had many safeguards in place to prevent hackers, and DDOS attacks. The members information was safe and this program would be around for a long time. He also declared they really didn't need any members but they decided to allow members to be able to join so they too could become wealthy.

Now if their claim that PT could mean anything you want it to mean didn't sound any alarms or you had bells and whistles going off, then you should have had them sounding when they claimed they were Internationalists/Sovereign Individuals, and saying they were not required to be licensed and registered anywhere. Now fast forward nine months and this is what Garrett Rainier had to say which was done in 2 parts. I have taken the most salient point from each part and put them together:

"Garrett Rainier:

Despite the naysayers, which I realize are many, and rightly so in some cases, I am here to update you all.

When PTV started, I had the best intentions of helping many. I envisioned at some point changing the ecurrency world. It was perhaps an overly grand vision. Actually, it might have worked had it not been for the circumstances that took place. Most will never know.

To list these reasons would open up a whole new debate and only be construed as excuses anyway. While the naysayers will tell you this is just more talk to keep members quiet, that is not the case.

When PTV started I believed I had taken all the necessary actions to keep any of the usual things from going wrong. On that the naysayers are right. I was wrong. Much happened and in trying to "fix" the problems more were created. Finally, at the end there was almost no way to adequately fix it. Not with the site running and not under the circumstances that were created.

The next part is the hardest to say. We have taken down the site completely but I have not gone away. I am here, licking my wounds a bit since, but with the full intention of paying all those not in profit. Those that were in profit, I am sorry but there is no way to continue paying out at this point on the plans that were running. The current steps that are being taken are these.

1) A full accounting has to be done. Because of all the issues that happened to the script and the errors that were made by some of the IT staff and the corrections we attempted that backfired we are unable to do this in a hurry. This is anticipated to be completed within a few weeks.

2) We are considering the future. My reaction at this moment is to payout those not in profit and walk away. Should anything further be considered, it will be extremely limited in membership and possibly not even offered to any current online members.

I am sorry. None of this is what I intended in the beginning. Nothing is yet fully determined as we must get through the current situation first. Then we will take a break, look at what we have and make a decision from there……"

"The End!

The end of all the problems that is. Our ecurrency will be replenished by Monday and all accounts will be completely paid in full. We want to thank all the members who have been so patient with this problem.

Gold Plan is almost full as well. We will be removing it from the website as soon as it is completely fulfilled. Members who have participated will be able to continue in this program. Those who have participated will need to set the auto reinvest to continue participation at whatever level they wish to continue at. The maximum you can Re-Invest is 53% of your original investment.

We will be going Private in a couple of weeks and actually cannot wait to be out of the limelight. The website will have a member's only entrance and all other information will be obscure unless a membership has previously been registered. All inactive accounts will be purged early next week. All members with more than 4 accounts will be required to merge those accounts. The ability to do this will be forthcoming.

We apologize for all the problems. Those of you that have lost faith in us, we understand and wish you well. Your funds will still be available for withdraw and you will receive them by Monday Night Tuesday Morning of next week."

Garrett

The only problem was all the refunds promised and the payments in the queue were not made. The site went down and Garrett has totally disappeared. The fate of all the HYIP's not taken down by the authorities. Millions of dollars was lost in this Ponzi. Despite all the warnings to the public this was a Ponzi and not to join, many failed to heed the warnings. Thankfully many did The one thing that stood out to me more so than all the other HYIPs was the others at least had the pretense of an investment vehicle that was supposed to be generating their returns. In this program you had no clue where the money they were supposedly making was coming from. It was all smoke and mirrors and to be honest was selling a dream of a lifestyle which was a total dream. Do I believe there is a group called the PT Group? Absolutely not, as it was all a lie.

Early in the book I mentioned that these conmen prey on the desperation of people in today's economic meltdown. This is a classic example of preying on this desperation. For a very little amount of money, you were promised the keys to financial freedom and wealth. When you have friends and family members joining, you join because you don't want to be left out, especially if they do get rich, and you didn't join. These conmen are not only good, they are very, very good. They can make you believe in whatever they want you to believe in.

Here's the difference between a HYI investment and a HYIP Program:

HIGH YIELD INVESTMENTS provide you:

- A prospectus of the investment;
- They are registered and licensed in every country in which they do business, and can be verified;
- They have a real physical address that can be verified as real;
- They have a real phone number that can be verified as real;
- They have a listing of the major principals of the firm, and they can be verified;
- They have a customer service hotline that is a real phone number of the company;
- You fund your account using a bank wire, or by check;
- You receive quarterly statements about your account showing all activity (all trades made on your behalf, both buy and sell with settlement prices) for the quarter, beginning and ending balances of your account;
- You receive confirmations of your trade(s) in writing within three days of the trade;
- They do not pay referral fees;
- They publish in financial trade magazines, and online financial websites;
- They don't have "Promoter's or Shills" touting the investment;
- Your investment is listed and traded on real market exchanges, and you can monitor your position(s) daily; and
- In real trading you will win some days, and lose on others. There is no stated rate of return, only projections given to you.

HIGH YIELD INVESTMENT PROGRAMS provides you nothing but hype:

- The vast majority of these programs do not show a physical address for the entity. When they do provide an address it is discovered to be a fake address:
- They do not have a phone number for you to call;
- You do not know who the people are behind the program. They must always remain a secret, or they use a fake name;
- They are not registered or licensed anywhere, while claiming to be;
- They only use offshore money exchangers for you to deposit your funds;
- They do not provide you with a prospectus;
- They do not provide you quarterly statements of your account;
- None of you investment are viewable on any trading exchange;
- You only know what they claim they are investing your money in, as there is never any proof provided;
- You never receive any confirmation of the trades made on your behalf;
- The admin rarely use their real names. Only a very select few have;
- Secrecy is of the utmost importance, and they claim there is a NDA (Non-Disclosure Agreement) trying to give it the air of legitimacy;
- They always claim they must stay below the radar of government agencies, or it could cause problems for the program and for the members;
- They never reveal how they make the promised rate of return for your investment;
- They have to have the ever present "Promoter's or Shills" for the program to get started and continue for as long as possible before collapsing;
- They never advertise in any reputable financial magazine or website;
- They provide referral fees so you will help gin the program; and
- They never provide any proof of their claims, returns on investment, or supportive documents proving they are real.

There are only High Yield Investments that are real. There are NO High Yield Investment Programs presented on the Internet that are real and legal. They are all Scams/Ponzi's. How can I protect myself from all these scams? How can I determine if they are real or a scam? Are there any signs I should be looking for to alert me it is a scam? Yes there is. Just follow our Red Flag Warnings and Due Diligence steps, which is next.

Red Flag Warnings & Due Diligence

When someone sees a red flag, they know it means to either stop or use extreme caution as danger lies ahead. The same holds true for investments. Red Flags in dealing with investments should be treated more like the flashing red lights and bells ringing at railroad crossing gates. It not only means danger lies ahead, it means stop cold and don't go any further. In investments, there are many issues that can be considered a red flag. Whether or not it is just one, several or all of them, you should stop and not invest. If you ignore them, you have a 100% chance of losing your money. So what are the red flags of investments? Here is a listing of the most serious ones:

- A company says that because they are an Internet company the standard rules of being licensed and registered does not apply to them.
- The company is basically anonymous as they use free website hosting, free E-mail services (Yahoo, Google, hotmail, g-mail, etc.) instead of paying for a secure website or having an E-mail address with the company's name in the address.
- Your contact person only has a first name and is using a free E-mail address, not one using the company name.
- The company has no physical address, phone number, or contact information of any kind.
- The company is saying the returns are high yield, but there is little or no risk.
- They say your principal (amount you give them) investment is "guaranteed," or they promise a "guaranteed" rate of return.
- They say they need to stay below the radar of law enforcement agencies.
- They say the investment is special that has only been available to the rich or wealthy until now.
- They say the program is only available to a select few.
- They say the program is a private investment and does not require to be licensed or registered.
- Failure to provide financial statements, a prospectus, or details of the investment.

- Any investment that requires only a small administrative fee, but promises a large return, i.e.: a $30 administrative fee, but will pay you $50,000.
- The program is promoted as finally allowing the little guy to obtain the same financial products that until now were only available to the rich or super wealthy.
- They claim the program is registered offshore (outside the United States), and therefore is not subject to the SEC Rules and Regulations. This is a myth.
- Any investment program that does not provide clear and detailed explanations of their investment products.
- The program is too difficult to explain in layman's terms.
- Promoter's claiming to be connected to "insiders" of the program.
- This is a 'chance-of-a-lifetime' opportunity.

DUE DILIGENCE

When one hears the words due diligence many think of highly technical questions one must ask, or they must have a high knowledge and understanding of investments. Nothing could be further from the truth.

Actually due diligence is using your common sense. It is just general questions that everyone should ask before investing in any program, no matter who is offering it. So let's break it down.

When you are asked to invest into any program, if it is a legal program (meaning licensed and registered with the proper authorities) they must provide you a prospectus. Don't let that word scare you. Prospectus just means it is a written document that outlines the investment, the risks involved, who is offering the product, their address, contact information, fund manager, the mission of the fund (what it is about), some projections, history of like-minded investments, and a projected return on investment. They are very long, can be very boring, and in many instances over the investor's head due to all the legal issues that must be disclosed.

Now that is the technical side of due diligence. Now let's examine the really simple things you can do and have performed enough due diligence to ensure you are investing in a legal investment.

1. Who is the company offering the investment?
2. What is their address, phone number, fax number, and E-mail?
3. Who do they show as the contact person (customer service), as well as their phone and E-mail, should you need assistance or if something goes wrong?
4. What are their hours of operation (is customer service only during a specific time frame, or is it 24 hours)?
5. If a program is being offered only through the Internet does not in itself make it fraudulent. What you must know is this: They must comply with all the rules 1-4 above. If you see high return with little or no risk, that is an immediate **red flag**. Also if they say they are doing business offshore, want to keep below the radar of law enforcement agencies, the program is a special program for a select few, or only the wealthy know about this type of investment....these are all major **red flags**.
6. Many will claim they are private programs, thus do not have to be registered. This is not totally true. A Private Investment does not have to be registered with the authorities, **BUT** they are limited to no more than 100 total investors or a specific dollar amount, and must comply with Reg D of the SEC. All other investment products have to be licensed and registered in every jurisdiction in which it is being offered for sale. No matter where in the world it is. Another **red flag**.
7. If they say the word "**guaranteed**" return is another **red flag**. You cannot guarantee an investment return except for CD's, Money Market accounts or Bonds/Bond Funds. Even these are for very specific periods of time.
8. Check for audited financial statements by a CPA firm, and the name of the CPA firm is shown with their contact information.
9. Many times they count on the hype and emotion of the moment for you to throw all common sense out the window and invest now. Remember: If it is that good of an investment now, it will still be just as good next week or next month, or next year. **Do not be pressured into investing without having the time to check it out.**

10. Ask your accountant or attorney about the investment. If you have neither, then talk to a securities broker about it. They will answer your questions, and you don't have to be a client of theirs to do so. Many will gladly offer help, as they realize you just might become a client of theirs if they do help you. Don't be intimidated into not asking others for guidance or assistance.

11. Make sure you fully understand what it is you are investing in. Do not be pressured into investing if your questions have not been answered. If you start feeling like you are being given the run around, it is a major **red flag** or another warning signal.

12. Never, ever invest more than you can afford to lose, no matter how much due diligence you have done. Real investments can and do lose money. There are no guarantees in an investment of always making money or a return on your investment other than CD's, Money Market Account or Bonds/Bond Funds.

13. If a prospectus states returns are generated from the buying and selling of companies, leasing contracts, etc., make sure they list the names of the companies that were bought and sold or leasing contracts. If the specific names are missing, this is another major **red flag**.

14. When a company that operates solely on the Internet tries to deflect any negativity of their program, one method is to bring up Enron or World Com as examples of people losing their money to "legal" companies. This is another **red flag**. What happened to Enron and World Com has nothing to do with them or their legality.

15. If the company provides bios of the people who comprise the management team, check them out to make sure the bios are true verifying employment and college(s) attended..

As you can see basic due diligence is not that hard to do, but if you follow our Red Flag Warnings and do these basic due diligence steps, they will save you from being taken or scammed out of your money. Now that you know what simple due diligence is, it shouldn't intimidate you anymore. But to be sure you never become a victim of a scam again, or for the first time, here's how they do it next.

THE SCAMMER & THE SCRIPTWRITER:

So where do they come up with all these programs and the content for their program? Well, there are scriptwriters from whom you purchase scripts. Many of these scams use the same format, they just change the name and a few items inside the script to make it look like it is a new program. Many scripts are just recycled over and over, but there are the occasional new scripts that will be used as a template for future scams. So you decide what type of program you want to offer, you find a scriptwriter to write it for you, or that has a draft already done he can change to meet your specifications, pay him for it, and you are good to go.

SETTING UP THE DOMAIN NAME & HOSTING OF THE WEBSITE:

Next you have to set up your domain name, and register your website so you can begin to offer your program to the public. Depending on how much money you are willing to pay, you can obtain a server and host that will make you completely anonymous so you cannot be traced.

But what if you want to appear as though your program has been around for a long time, like three years or more, rather than just starting the program, can this be done? Of course, and here's how they do it:

What you do is purchase a domain name and park it for three years. You also sign up with the various payment processors all at the same time, because you don't know which ones will still be around three years later. This gives you a low account number with each payment processor. Then when you are ready to start your program, you dust off your domain name, buy your script, and take your program live. Thus when anyone does a search of the domain name, it will show that your domain name has been registered for three years, but in reality you just started offering your program. You claim you have been in business for three years, but are just now making your program available to the public on the Internet, and your domain registration supports this claim. It makes people believe you have longevity. Then you get people who are known to promote a program to join you, they will post extolling the virtues of your program, and how long it has been operating. This is how you fool people into believing your story-line you have been in business for three years. It makes people feel more secure in joining the program.

Ok, now I have my script, I have my domain name, host, and my server, how do I get noticed on the financial forums when there are so many other programs already being promoted on them?

LIST OWNERS

There are networks of people who continually promote such programs. At a higher level, they include "list owners" who distribute information via e-mail, their own private forums, blogs, etc., to their members. If you look you will see they tend to come through the same groups. The people behind these scams know where to go to get their programs into the networks in order for them to get promoted widely, just as they know where to go for complete anonymous hosting, anonymous payment systems, and bank accounts.

THE ONLINE FINANCIAL NEWSLETTER REPORTER

You do an interview with an online "so-called reporter" to help introduce your program and for them to bless your program with their recommendation. The interview is pre-scripted and all questions are softball ones so your program is presented in the best possible light. No questions are allowed as to where you are licensed and registered to do business, and if you are in compliance with all regulatory agencies where you will be doing business. Nor will you be asked your address, phone number any license or registration numbers. Of course you pay them for this interview, and of course most get a front-line position in your program. The list promoters will provide links to the interview to give the program the air of legitimacy, and to hype interest in joining the program as it launches. You do the same thing with the financial forums where you purchase advertising of your program. Of course the reporter who conducted the interview always have glowing remarks about your program, and the obligatory this one looks like it will be around a long, long time.

THE FINANCIAL FORUMS

So how do they get listed on the financial forums? Like the scriptwriter and the promoter's, the owners of the financial forums are paid to promote the program. The owners sell advertising space on the forum so when people come to the sites, they will see your ads, and then check out your program. Now the Ponzi shill and the promoter have started posting how great your program is, and all the usual glowing remarks that entices others to join. Next to join the chorus of how wonderful your program is and extolling the virtues of your program are the people in the down-line of the promoter. Suddenly the thread for your program is exploding with glowing comments and urging people not to miss the boat on this sure-fire winner and sign-up now. With all these testimonials come the obligatory "I got paid," "Paid Instantly," "They have never missed a payment," "This is one of the better ones paying," "Always paid on time as promised," you get the idea. Soon thousands have joined, and before long it is in the tens of thousands if not hundreds of thousands. This is how these scams get started and flourish for a time before they either collapse or are raided by the feds. Before in the HYIP world a program could last close to 18 months before folding; but not today. Today they are lucky to last nine months, in spite of what I have just explained how they work.

While you are doing this, you also contact several individuals who are known "promoters" of these scam investment programs. Usually these are people who have a large down-line of people who follow them from program to program. You get as many of these promoters as you can, because the more people you have joining, and posting about the greatness of your program; the faster your program will catch on and the money will be rolling in. The majority of the time these promoters are given guarantees their investment will be returned with a stated percentage of profit. They will receive higher referral fees on everyone they get signed up in the program compared to regular referral fee for the members. Here's the secret. Almost all promoters are in and out of the program before the masses have joined, yet they make claims they are still being paid when they are no longer in the program. The only thing they are being paid is their referral fees. To the public it appears they are still invested, and thus they join.

PONZI SHILLS

There are many different levels of "insiders" in the HYIP Ponzi business. One of the layers are the ones we call the Ponzi shills who don't get paid directly like the others, but instead are paid by being given early positions in the program, or are paid by being given higher referral commissions. They are the ones who also make the initial post about a program on the financial forums. So they can change hats to play whatever role they are paid to play. Their job is to pretend to be the average investor who joined the program just like everyone else, but praises the program and encourages others to join and not miss the boat on this sure-fire winner. They claim they have checked the program out and they found nothing wrong.

THE MODS

Another layer of the players in this Ponzi business are the mods (short for moderator) of the private forum of the program. Their job is to answer all questions from the membership, and help them resolve payment issues, deposit issues, back-office issues, etc, etc. But their main job is to maintain order and not let the members get out of line by asking tough questions and demanding answers no-one is willing to give. Then they can become dictatorial in their role. They have been known to threaten people they will not get paid if they continue to cause trouble; or they will have their accounts closed and not receive their payments. They will ban people from the forum they think are trouble-makers. These bans can last for a few hours, to a day, a week or longer. They are there to protect the admin/owner of the program from all negative comments about the program or the admin on the private forum. They are who we also call the gate-keepers.

The financial forums also have mods, whose job is to keep civility on the threads for each of the investment programs being discussed. They too can become dictatorial in their control of the forum. Many times they are in the scam program they are acting as a mod for on the forum. So not exactly unbiased, and they can ban people, put people on mod review which means a post will not be posted on the forum until a mod has looked at it and determined it is OK to be posted. They can request it be modified and then they will post it, or they do not let the post be made at all. Of course they claim a person was banned for calling people names, using vulgarity, threatening people, all of which are legitimate reasons for having a person banned. The problem is many times the only people being banned are those exposing the scam. The promoters and the shills can say just about anything about the "Naysayer or Troll," the ones who challenge the program and exposing it as a scam, without being banned. One of the promoters and shills weapons is to try and discredit a Naysayer or Troll. Remember when I said the mod may have a position in the scam, and here is where their bias comes into play? They can also close a thread to new posts if they feel the program is under too much attack as a scam, and they want to protect it from further exposure. So they have a lot of power, and many times it does go to their head. I would not want to be a mod whether they paid me or not. Not all mods are control freaks or rule with an iron hand. There are some very good mods who allow the discussions to occur as long as they remain civil and stay on topic. They are just too few and far between.

THE PROMOTERS

Their counter-part on the public forums are the promoters of the program. Their job is a little harder as they do not have censorship powers like the mods on the private forum; but their job is the same: to protect the program and admin at all costs. They are to discredit anyone who dares challenge the programs integrity, legality and exposing the program as a scam/Ponzi. They need to keep people joining, and they do their best to deflect any criticism or the legality of the program. They also are helping to keep the members believing in the program and not to listen to anyone exposing or challenging the program. They always point to all the people posting "I've Got Paid," as the program being legitimate. This is their version of due diligence. What they also didn't tell you is that most of them are fake claims they were paid, and for those who were, they were paid in advance to post "I've Got Paid." Yes, there are some who really did get paid, for if they didn't the whole program would collapse. It is the latter stages of the program when these claims of I got paid become suspect to being faked.

The promoters are also given special positions, and special referral fees not given to the standard member. These promoters usually have a large down-line of people that follow them from scam-to-scam because they are in early and out early thus making money. The promoters are guaranteed a rate of return for investing that is higher than what is offered to the regular member. In essence, they get special treatment at every turn of the scam. Higher rates of return, higher referral fees, and of course their investment is guaranteed so they never lose money. That's why they go from scam-to-scam as it is easy money for them.

As mentioned, the promoters role is to protect the program for as long as possible so they can make as much as possible before the program folds. They do this by trying to discredit the people who are challenging the program. These challengers are called "Trolls," "Naysayers," "Negative People," "People who are Jealous," "People who are Crusaders/Do-Gooder's," and those are just the nice names. Their tactics vary from Troll/Naysayer to Troll/Naysayer but here are a few examples, and these are all direct quotes from the Financial Forums:

"What is your hidden agenda?" "What difference does it make if a person wants to participate in the program for they do have 'freedom of choice" don't they?""Who are you to tell them what they can and can't do?" "What's it to you, it's their money". "We are all adults and we don't need babysitters"." "No-one needs you to tell them what to do, and besides who appointed you to tell them what they should do?" "You say this program is illegal, so where is your "Proof" it isn't?"

"Obviously the reason they likely do not want the likes of you to know the exact facts as to their real name and location should be clear to even you.......they don't trust you to handle this info in an honest manner." "Just because they stated something in their website does not necessarily make it a fact." " Did it ever cross your tiny mind that in the financial arena that they function in, they do not need to register with SEC and do not have to reveal their licensing." " You might want to consider that these "so-called" excuses are legitimate delays faced by ALL business ventures". " As for "secret" investment arrangements......there have been these around the world for decades and many multi-billion dollar consortiums have used these over and over. They are legal and are structured so that many of the normal rules of investment do not apply".

"When you come right down to it no one was forced to invest their money. We did it all ourselves hoping to make the big bucks. But the bottom line is, we knew we were taking a risk." "I am sick of processors making scape goats out of honest people and honest admins.""You can't call this a scam because only the courts can. What happened to a person is presumed to be innocent? You have already tried him and found him guilty. Only a court of law can do that." "Once you get the authorities involved even with legit programs they can make havoc of the programs. and please don't come back with the response that if they are legit, they don't have to worry. That's a bunch of crap to."" Personally I'm hoping for Nick to turn the tables on these jerks who take down honest programs.......I notice that they never touch the scam programs.........why is that.......oh yes, that's because there's no money to be gotten from a scam program."

I think these give you a good idea of who the promoters and mods do all they can to protect the admin and the program. Never mind they are the ones who are required to provide "Proof" the program is legal. You cannot prove a negative. They believe if they can discredit you, others will not pay attention to you, and one of the best ways to do this is make people think you have a hidden agenda you are not willing to let people know about. It is called deflection from the real issues. Another tactic they use is to never answer any of your questions by either ignoring the questions, or direct the attention to something that has no bearing on the questions asked. The reason they do this is because they cannot answer the question, and to do so would prove the program is a Ponzi. They are almost as good at playing the smoke and mirror game, as the scammer is making you believe his program is legal, and going to make you rich. It is all smoke and mirrors.

When the above tactics do not seem to be working, then we have the standard government conspiracy theory is trotted out by one or more of the promoters. Trying to convince people the scam is no different than the scam run by the government. *The first claim is that Social Security is a Ponzi, so why aren't you going after it?* When this fails, they up the ante to other government entities are scams and their argument goes something along these lines:

"Since you are so adamant about going after scams, when are you going after the SEC receiver/scam artists who rake in millions 'protecting' our interests?"

"Are they cutting you in when your diligence in protecting us by reporting companies you have decided are scamming us pays off and they shut them down and steal everyone's money?"

"You believe that receivers deserve millions while participants receive pennies on the dollar, you do not see that SS is a Ponzi (uses new money to pay out oldest members and does not earn enough to do this without using the newest members' funds)."

"You have never once participated in a program presented here other than to immediately report it once you see it."

"As is the case with mainstream investments, we get to see what we are wanted to see regardless of how diligent our research is."

"The foreclosure fiasco and the Wall St. meltdown are indicative of this."

"Just because something has been legitimized by the US Crime Machine doesn't mean it is ethical, moral or legitimate in the ideal. It simply means that educated people in suits have created loopholes to make themselves appear as if they have the public's interest in mind as they pilfer our earnings."

We are to demand accountability from the government agencies, but not the scammer who is stealing your money. Not once do they claim the scammer should be caught and go to prison, or be required to give the money back.

Also in this HYIP world you can have a scam inside a scam. Many times the scammer behind his program will also invest in someone else's program, and of course they get special and preferential treatment for doing so. Their investment is guaranteed with a stated percentage of interest. This allows the people behind these programs to make even more money off the unsuspecting public as they don't know these deals are going on behind the scenes. Just like the special shills, promoters, reporters, and owners of the forums were being paid without the public's knowledge. Well up until now you didn't.

But this you can take to the bank, that on every financial forum where these illegal programs are listed and promoted, as Patrick Pretty of patrickpretty.com blog so aptly put it, there will be someone posting as follows and I quote:

"There will be a promoter(s) railing against the government, railing against the posters who are trying to expose and educate the public about such scams, and the lengths they promoter will go to sanitize the schemer and rationalize their behavior.

There will be a promoter(s) railing against the court-appointed receiver, and falsely accusing the receiver's goal is greed. Never mind the scammer was the one who created the situation that caused the requirement for a court-appointed receiver in the first place. That the receiver will spend countless hours unraveling and reverse engineering the scam, and it is a costly, time-consuming process.

They will do their best to sanitize their and the scammers role in causing the financial nightmare in the first place."

By the time the masses have joined is when the program is about to implode or the feds are going to shut them down. There are only two ways a program ends: 1. They are raided by the Feds, or 2. They disappear and have run with the money.

THE PLAYERS

There are those who are not promoters, but who we call the "Players." These are people who think all of this is a game, and therefore if you don't know how to play the game, you should not invest. They see nothing wrong in taking advantage of those who are called 'newbies' – first time investors in these scams. For the newbies think they are real investments, the program will not collapse and they will lose all their money. The players know the game is played by getting in early and getting out early. They only stay in long enough to recover their principal, plus a little return and then they are out of the program. Or if a program has a roll-over aspect, they pull out their principal and play on the 'houses' money, so to speak, from new members joining the program. Thus they have not lost anything, and are making money off their interest as long as the program pays.

The only problem is that the programs are never presented as a "game," but instead as an "investment" opportunity. Now if the admin would post on their programs website in bold letters "THIS IS A GAME," then the players may have a point. But they don't. They never say this is a game. They also say you should never invest more than you can afford to lose, which is true. But this is always mentioned after the program has collapsed, not before.

No matter what type of investment you invest in, you should never invest money needed for your mortgage, car payment, utilities, groceries, and other living expenses. It should always be "disposable income," meaning if you lose it the loss will not affect your standard of living. The day the programs start putting THIS IS A GAME on their websites, then I will agree it is just a "GAME." Actually I think this disclaimer should be put on every HYIP programs website in bold, red, giant, all-capital letters:

Your cost to join this program constitutes the minimum contract, not including applicable taxes and license fees, fuel surcharges, telephone charges, leather goods, flippers and mask, vegetable oil, marital aids, anesthetics, or tissue. Must be 9 years of age or older to participate. Offer does not comply with the laws of the United States, Canada, United Kingdom, France, Germany, Sweden, Norway, Denmark, Belgium, Holland, Italy, Spain, India, China, Russian Federation, Singapore, Indonesia, Australia, New Zealand, Antarctica, Japan, Korea, Brazil, Chile, Argentina, Uruguay, Ecuador, Venezuela, Bahamas, Mexico, Panama, Costa Rica, Belize, Somalia, or Vanuatu. No implication, promise or guarantee of wealth is included in this offer. For additional information consult your astrologer. All sales are final.

Yes, I am being facetious, but I think you get the message. Whether you are a mod, promoter, shill, or player, if you call them games, you are merely deluding yourself and trying to assuage your conscious by embracing a psychology that lets you off the hook for the pain you end up causing to both people you know and strangers alike. While you may claim you are embracing "freedom of choice, " and only the rare few don't know HYIPs are "games," you reveal yourself as a pusher of pain and suffering just like a drug dealer does.

THE PAYMENT PROCESSORS

But the most important player in all of this are the Payment Processors. They offer their money exchange services for a fee. The scammer does not want a money trail following him, so instead of using bank wires or checks like investment firms, they use payment processors. The biggest payment processors used are located in Canada. While there are other payment processors, the Canadian payment processors are those of choice by the scammers. Since the payment processors they use are outside the borders of the U.S., they are called offshore payment processors. The payment processors are the currency exchangers for these programs. They make it possible for people all over the world, regardless of the currency they use, to participate in these HYIP programs. They charge both parties (the program admin and the members) fees for their investment in the program and for their payments from the program. Without the payment processors, this whole industry would come crashing down.

THE OFFSHORE MYTH

The last ploy used by the people behind these scams, and the promoters is the claim that having an offshore registration, meaning foreign country, exempts the investment from having to comply and be registered with the SEC (Securities & Exchange Commission) and not subject to federal law enforcement agencies. Along with this claim comes the we are operating online, therefore, we are not subject to any laws and government regulations or law enforcement agencies. This is a myth. The truth is that if just one U.S. citizen is solicited and is an investor in any investment program, no matter where it is registered, the investment must be registered with the SEC and in every state where they are doing business. U.S. law enforcement agencies do have jurisdiction.

Illustrating the fallacy of this myth Nick Smirnow, a Canadian citizen, was running an offshore program called Pathway-To-Prosperity (P2P for short), or as many of us called it Pathway-To-Poverty. This program collapsed and charges were filed by the Canadian authorities, and an arrest warrant was issued. Nick and his wife had fled to the Philippines prior to the Canadian charges being filed. So what does this have to do with P2P needing to be registered and licensed with the SEC? Nick was offering his program to U.S. citizens as well as citizens from countries all around the world. He also claimed because he was offshore, he was not subject to the U.S. SEC rules and regulations, nor having to be registered in any U.S. state in which he was accepting investors, and not subject to U.S. law enforcement agencies. Well, the U.S. filed charges against him and they are seeking extradition from the Philippine government for his return to stand trial here in the U.S.

So much for not being subject to U.S. securities laws and subject to U.S. law enforcement agencies as claimed. A myth that has very clearly been exposed as a lie within the last few months with the U.S. authorities extraditing individuals who were running scams against U.S. citizens from Jamaica, Argentina, France, Thailand, Colombia, and Panama to name but a few. We know that more will be extradited in the near future. The message is being sent it makes no difference where you are, or what country you are operating out of, if you accept U.S. citizens as investors in your program you are not exempt from the SEC rules and regulations. The U.S. authorities will come and get you to stand trial for your crimes.

My observations from researching and studying these scams over the past seven years:

- Sell people hope. People live on hope, and their hopes and dreams must be fed through spin and lies. In any situation, if possible, accentuate the positive.
- Make excuses as long as you can. Try to have your excuses based on at least one truthful fact even if the fact is unrelated to your actions and argument.
- When you cannot dispute the underlying facts, accept them as true but rationalize your actions. You are allowed to make mistakes as long as you have no wrongful intent. Being stupid is not a crime.

- Always say in words you "take responsibility" but try to indirectly shift the blame on other people and factors. You need to portray yourself as a "stand up" guy or gal.
- When you cannot defend your actions or arguments attack the messenger to detract attention from your questionable actions.
- Always show your kindness by doing people favors. You will require the gratitude of such people to come to your aid and defend you.
- Build up your stature, integrity, and credibility by publicizing the good deeds you have done in areas unrelated to the subject of scrutiny.
- Build a strong base of support. Try to have surrogates and the beneficiaries of your largess stand up for you and defend you.
- If you can, appear to take the "high road" and have your surrogates do the "dirty work" for you. After all, you cannot control the actions of your zealots.
- Blame others inside your organization by claiming they were doing things they were not authorized to do; or operated outside of their authority you had given them to act.
- Claim your organization has been given a clean bill of health by the governing authorities.
- Claim your statements have been taken out of context or twisted by critics not wanting the organization to succeed.
- Blame your problems on jealous competitors, banks or financial institutions, or overzealous government agencies trying to keep the little guy down.
- When you can no longer spin, shut up. For example, offer no guidance to investors or resign for "personal reasons." Your surrogates and so-called friends can still speak on your behalf and defend you.
- If you are under investigation always say you will "cooperate." However, use all means necessary legal or otherwise to stifle the investigators. Remember that "people live on hope" and their inclination is to believe you.
- When called to testify under oath (if you do not exercise your 5th amendment privilege against self-incrimination) have selective memory about your questionable actions. It is harder to be charged with perjury if you cannot remember what you have done rather than testify and lie about it.

- However, before you testify have other friendly witnesses testify before you to defend you. You need to "lock in" their stories first (before they change their minds) so your testimony does not conflict with their testimony and your story will appear to be more truthful.
- Try not to have your actions at least appear to rise to the level of criminal conduct or a litigable action. Being stupid or being unethical is not always a crime or a tortuous action.
- One last rule, to be a most effective spinner always keep your friends close and your enemies closer. The kindness you show your enemies will reduce their propensity to be skeptical of you.

Now here is how they set it all up, and what most don't know is many times they are running multiple scams at the same time. They just use different names for the admin, but they are one and the same person. So if you are in invested in more than one Internet HYIP investment program, the odds are you are probably being scammed by the same scammer and you don't even know it:

- They obtain fake documents. For about $200 they can get documents that look as good as the real ones, if not better.
- They rent an apartment, usually in a beachside community with a fast Internet service, and a nice view.
- They open a bank account with their fake documents, and obtain a debit card.
- They then open accounts with several payment processors using some of the money from the bank account referenced above.
- They make up a name for the company, no real registration required of any kind.
- They set up their domain registration and E-mail accounts with companies that will protect them from being found when doing a search keeping them totally anonymous.
- They can withdraw large sums of money through purchasing hundreds of special cards, which they give to their family and friends, allowing them to withdraw money from any ATM anywhere on a daily basis that does not have a $800 withdrawal limit per day.

- And of course the payment processors who will send $200,000 to $300,000 every three days to their bank account under their fake name.
- To make sure the money exchangers will work with them, they offer double their normal fee for allowing their "privacy" to be protected.
- Many of the scams are planned up to three years in advance before launching to give the air of longevity.
- They have bought their script, obtained the host for their website, and they open for business.
- It is safer than robbing a bank. The average bank robber only gets away with a couple of thousand of dollars, but an Internet scammer gets away with tens of millions of dollars if not hundreds of millions of dollars, and NO GUN IS REQUIRED.

If you are a promoter of these scams, or if you are one of the people who go from scam-to-scam claiming you are just playing the game because you know to get in early and get out fast, you can be charged with a misprision of a felony. What is misprision of a felony? Here is how "misprision of felony" reads under Section 4 of the U.S. Code:

"Whoever, having knowledge of the actual commission of a felony cognizable by a court of the United States, conceals and does not as soon as possible make known the same to some judge or other person in civil or military authority under the United States, shall be fined under this title or imprisoned not more than three years, or both."

HOW DO PEOPLE FALL FOR THESE SCAMS?

The people who run these scams, as I have said before, are sociopaths in my opinion with a dose of Narcissism thrown in for good measure; as are the promoters of these scams. They do it with the typical sales tactics we are all familiar with. They are enthusiastic about their program. They have testimonials from people who are just like you praising the honesty of the admin and how great the program is, and you will not go wrong in joining. They are there to answer any of your questions, they make themselves available at all times, they tell you about their background growing up, how they just want to help the average person get ahead in life; all the things designed to lower your guard and make you feel like you have known this person all your life. They make you comfortable with them and your decision to join their program, when in fact you have no clue who they really are, and know nothing about them.

They convince you they have designed a new program that 'guarantees' your principal, but is different than the typical investment program. In fact they are the only ones who know how it works. A broker, CPA/accountant, financial planner is only trained in the traditional products, and therefore does not understand how their program works. So their advice cannot be relied upon when checking out this program. They do the same thing with saying bankers do not want to admit these programs exist because they do not want the masses to know about them. They convince you they are the only ones who know the truth, and they are the only ones you can rely on. If it doesn't come from them, it is not the truth.

They also tell you not to pay attention to anyone who disagrees with or challenges the program as being legitimate. They are: negative people, jealous, don't understand the program, trouble-makers...you get the drift. These are people you don't want to be around or pay attention to because they will drag you down. They don't want you getting ahead in life, but refuse to take the risk to get ahead themselves. This in ingrained into your psyche as part of your participation in their program. Their private forum becomes your social network, and without your realizing it, you have become part of a cult-like behavior group. You will not accept anyone who is not part of the program, or what they have to say.

Now when I point out on the financial forums people who join these programs are in a cult-like group, they go ballistic. No-one wants to claim or admit to being part of a cult, and they profess vigorously they are not in a cult. I did not say they were in a cult, but they are in a cult-like group. In a cult, the only one who knows the truth is the leader. All outside contact is prohibited. Anyone who challenges the group is not enlightened and does not know the truth. You are not allowed to challenge the leader. Most of these elements are exactly what happens inside the membership of these scams. Only the admin knows how the program works. Anyone who challenges the admin or the program is not to be believed. Dissent is not allowed.

Bryan Marsden, of PIPS fame, made an around the world tour where he made presentations in many major cities. At these meetings, no dissent was allowed of the program or of him. He could look you in the eye and tell you the biggest lie and people believed him. What was even more bizarre is the further he went into the tour, the bigger the lies became and the easier it was for the members to believe it. By the time he did his Hawaii meeting, PIPS had only made selective payments to a very few people, but had not paid the majority of the members for five months. Despite all of this, he announced PIPS was forming its own bank, and the crowd went wild. You see it was all the bank's fault he was unable to pay people what they were owed. So this was to solve this problem. It was all a lie. Remember, sociopaths can look you in the eye, lie, and make you believe it is the truth; because they believe what they said was not a lie.

Andy Bowdoin, of ASD fame, also held rally's in major US cities to which thousands attended. After attending one you felt as if you had just come from an old-fashioned tent revival meeting of the 50s-60s. Just like Byran Marsden, as each rally was held, the lies increased and the members bought it. In fact he claimed he was going to make 100,000 millionaires through ASD, and the crowd went wild with cheers. The bigger the lie, the easier it was to sell it. Andy met with people at each of these events, looked them in the eye, and lied to everyone of them and they believed him.

Nothing is ever the admin's fault. It is always outside forces that are working against him. Whether it is the banks, naysayers, payment processors, hackers, DDOS attacks, and yes even the members themselves are the problem not the admin.

To keep control of the private forum, if anyone starts asking any difficult questions, or challenges the admin, immediately the member is told to stop it or they will be removed from being paid. Now stop and think about this for just a moment. It is your money that you invested in this program, but if you dare ask any questions or challenge what is being done you run the risk of not receiving your payment. What do you think you would do if your banker said to you: "I don't like your questions about your CD, and if you don't stop, you won't get paid."? The problem is with the investment program the members on the private forum stopped asking questions for fear of not being paid. Intimidation works well for the admin and they know it.

People have been so ingrained with the storyline of the admin that even when the admin was arrested, the members believed the program was not a scam and the authorities just got it wrong. No-one likes to admit they were scammed. You just don't want to believe it, and sadly many don't accept it for a long time. To prove my point after the asset seizure by the Secret Service, the members of ASD were writing letters to Congressmen, Senators, the Inspector General, the president, and others all complaining the government had overstepped their bounds by seizing ASD's assets. They had a right to free commerce with whomever they wanted. They wanted the attorney for the government fired as he did not understand the business model of ASD. The government acted illegally in seizing ASD assets. They wrote letters of support to Andy, sent him cakes, cookies, brownies (I'll give you my address if you will send me brownies especially if laced with chocolate chips and chocolate icing), cards all praising him. They considered a march on Washington, and many other things trying to defend Andy and ASD. Totally refusing to believe they were part of an illegal Ponzi program, and anyone exposing ASD as a Ponzi.

Andy Bowdoin has challenged the asset seizure in court. When the asset seizure was made, Andy had his attorney file for an emergency Evidentiary hearing. Andy had told the faithful that all he needed to do was to explain the ASD business model in court, and the government would drop the asset seizure. The government did not contest this Evidentiary hearing. Now remember, Andy demanded this hearing so he could explain the ASD business model. When the hearing was held, Andy notified the court he would not testify, but would take the 5th if called to do so. When those of us who were exposing ASD as a Ponzi referenced Andy's failure to testify after claiming he couldn't wait to explain how the ASD business model was not a Ponzi, one of his supporters said, and I quote: "Andy was too honest to testify." No I did not make that up. Here Andy got caught in a major lie, and as the faithful were trained, refused to believe it and gave an excuse for his lie.

Now you have seen the: who, what, how and where:

- Who all the players are;
- What each role each one has to play;

- How they make a program appear to have been around longer than it really has;
- Who gets paid and how, behind the scenes;
- Where the content of the programs comes from;
- How they keep themselves anonymous as much as possible;
- How the game is stacked against the unknowing public; and
- How people fall for these scams.

You now realize how millions of dollars are stolen daily. Now you should never become a victim of a scam.

One other element about these scams is this: Because of the large amount of money that moves through these scams, you never know where the return of your investment is coming from. For all you know it could be from laundering drug money. It is possible that organizations join these scams to clean dirty money, use their returns to fund terrorism, child trafficking, pornography, the sex-trade, or any other illegal business. The truth is it could be for all of them. The people running these scams do not care where the money is coming from as long as it is coming. They do not check to see who the member is, or the source of his funds. They leave that to the payment processor, and many times they are not as diligent as they should be when they process the payments being made to them from the members joining the program.

What you must remember is that at best 15% make money from these scams, which means 85% lose their money. Sometimes it is as little as 5%, but the vast majority will lose everything they invest. Just because someone makes a post on a financial forum saying "I got paid," does not mean they really did get paid, and it is not due diligence. Many times the "I got paid" statements are just that statements. The only type of scam that people do not get paid are those involving a future event happening (GPP) before payments will be made. The only problem is the future event never happens and no-one gets paid. Everyone loses their money.

WARNING SIGNS YOUR PROGRAM IS ABOUT TO CLOSE

If you happen to be in an Internet investment scam, here are the early warning signs your program is about to close:

1. Payments that were always on time are suddenly a day or two late;
2. They make up an excuse as to why payments cannot be made immediately;
3. They blame the payment processors for the delay in payments;
4. They start making "selected" payments;
5. The promoters suddenly disappear from the financial forums;
6. They change the plan by announcing they are increasing the minimum investment and decreasing the rate of return;
7. They blame the members for taking advantage of the referral system, and they have to close the referral program and do an audit;
8. You cannot access the website for an extended period of time with no explanation;
9. They claim they were under DDOS attack, when there were no problems before;
10. They say the database was hacked;
11. They need to transfer the database to a new server and there are script problems creating delays in paying;
12. Suddenly all payments stop, and all withdrawal requests are not honored with no warning or explanation;
13. They announce they need to take the program private, and announce a future date when this will happen;
14. They claim there have been delays in wiring funds from their bank account to the payment processors to make payments that are beyond their control;
15. They announce they are working diligently to resolve all these issues, but cannot give a timeline when they will be resolved; and
16. The admin stops posting on the private forum, and stops all personal communication.

These events usually happen in a sequence, but can happen in clusters. The bottom line is they all indicate the program is running out of money to keep the scam going. Well, at least what they want to pay to the members. They have the money, they just don't want to pay it back to you.

If any of these events start happening, get out as fast as you can, because it is going to collapse unless the feds raid it first. But in all of this there is a dark side that no-one wants to talk about, nor will you see it mentioned on any of the financial forums, or discussed in any of the 'interviews' conducted by the online financial news reporters. Nest, the Dark Side of Investment Scams. The real result of being caught up in these scams.

The Dark Side of Investment Scams

The one subject rarely discussed on any of the financial forums is what happens to people who lose all of their money, life savings, retirement income, college fund, 401(K) funds, borrowed money, or charged their investment to their credit cards in these scams. This is the dark side of investment scams and it is ugly. These scams are portrayed as harmless, and cause no serious consequences if they fail. They don't talk about it because it helps them assuage their conscious they have done nothing wrong. Nothing could be further from the truth. Here are a few examples of what I am talking about and I quote:

"I was shown how to use apparent scams and make money before they go down and since I DO NOT refer anyone to any program, I hurt no one."

"IF I was wrong in what I am accomplishing, I might consider that, but since I have made huge sums myself and have helped others to do the same."

"We all are adults and know how the game is played. Each person is responsible for their actions, not me. If they invested more than they should have, it is not my fault."

"People should not play the game if they don't know the consequences, and it is not job to babysit them."

"I was able to make money, but was fooled like everyone else. Just because I made money is not my fault others didn't. Don't play if you don't know the rules of the game."

"Why should I feel guilty about someone else's mistakes? I didn't force them to join. They did it of their own free will. It is called 'freedom of choice, ' we all have."

I receive phone calls almost weekly from people who have become victims of these scams, and the trials and tribulations they are facing. Yes, they should not have invested their life savings, borrowed money, taken out a second mortgage on their house, or invested their 401(K) or IRA money; but the facts are they did. Not only were they seeking advice on what they should do next, but they needed to tell their story to someone who would not judge them to help reduce their guilt and stress. Here are just a few of the horror stories I have been told. These stories are more detailed and complex than presented, but are summarized for brevity and privacy. All have requested to remain anonymous, but their stories are true:

Story 1:

A very dear friend of mine joined an MLM Program that was involved in providing an energy saving product, or so they claimed. Prior to joining, he spoke with the programs legal counsel, as well as others in the program asking a lot of questions. After speaking with everyone, he was convinced the program was legal primarily from the information of the legal counsel professing they were a legitimate company.

He jumped in with both feet. He only wanted to provide a little extra income for his family on a monthly basis so they would not be so tight financially. Believing it was legal, he recruited others to join the program to follow his example. It was not long until he was promoted to Regional Manager, and had people from three states under him. Things were good, and he was making much needed extra income. This income grew to about a couple of thousand dollars total. All was well with the world. He thought bigger and better things were to come, and his income would grow with it.

Then the bottom fell out. The company folded and he was arrested on a federal felony warrant for his participation in this scam. He willingly assisted the U.S. Attorney with their case by providing all his correspondence and E-mails, and testifying against the principals aiding in their conviction. Having done all that the U.S. Attorney still wanted him to serve federal prison time for his role. Fortunately he was able to reach a plea deal, was sentenced to house arrest which required him to wear an ankle monitoring bracelet, and then be placed on parole at the end of his house arrest. He lost his professional licenses and will have a federal felony conviction on his record for life. Think it can't happen to you, think again.

Story 2:

I received a phone call from a person who had just found out that the company he had invested he and his wife's life-savings had gone bust, losing it all. He wanted to know what, if anything, could be done to try and get any of it back. This loss was placing his marriage on the brink of divorce, and they were hanging on financially by a thread. His wife was making him out to be as bad as the person that scammed them. He didn't know if they would ever recover from this loss emotionally, financially, and relationally. It was also affecting his and his wife's health. He felt all trust was gone and she would never trust him again. By the way, this was an educated and professional man. Think it can't happen to you, think again.

Story 3:

A call was received from a woman whose husband had just committed suicide from losing all their life's savings to a scam artist. She didn't know what to do or who to turn to for help. She had no money, and she was about to lose their home of 25 years as she could not afford to pay the mortgage. To compound the problem, since he committed suicide, she would not receive the double-indemnity clause for accidental death as suicide is not an accident. The amount of life insurance she will receive will barely cover the expenses of his funeral and possibly estate taxes owed. Hopefully this will never happen to you or a loved one.

Story 4:

I was contacted by a man who said he was a victim of a scam, and not only did his wife divorce him, but those who he referred into the scam were all suing him civilly to recover their losses. He had to sell everything he owned for the divorce settlement, and now did not know how he would be able to pay back all those he referred into the program if he lost the civil cases. If you think this can't happen to you, think again.

Story 5:

Another person posted on one of the financial forums that he suffered from chronic back pain and had lost the sight in one eye, and intermittent problems in his good eye. His wife had suffered from depression, and through expensive treatments was showing some progress when the investment program they were in stopped paying. All the progress she had made prior to this happening was immediately lost, and her depression worsened. Even with his back pain, he has to lift her in and out of bed, chairs and the bathroom facilities. He joined the program because of a personal friend whom he trusted had invested. Everyone he knew had put in considerable amounts of money in the program just prior to it folding. Because of this, he now watches his wife deteriorate each and every day. They had to close her personal business due to her deep depression, and it added even more of a toll on her health, as well as his. Since they can no longer afford the medical treatment, it is unclear what her health status will be in the next few months provided she continues to deteriorate daily.

Story 6:

Received contact from an individual who said like others that were caught up in a scam that he now has been ostracized by his family, cut-off from the family inheritance, and struggling to keep his marriage from falling apart. His grown children have also distanced themselves from him, and have told him he is not welcome in their homes. Not only did he lose communication with his children, but cannot see his grandchildren, all because of a poor investment decision. While he is still young enough to recoup most of what he lost, he is not sure with all the economic uncertainty today if he will even have a job to do so. Fearing a heart attack, his doctor is treating him for high blood pressure, hypertension, stress, and depression. His wife is receiving treatment for her depression, and they are receiving marriage counseling in hope of saving their marriage. He doesn't know what he will do if they cannot. Don't let this happen to you.

Story 7:

I received a call from a man who has a professional license. He had to tell his ailing elderly grandmother and parents that he had lost their life savings in a scam. While he said it would cause him and his wife financial difficulty, he would be able to cover their losses over time. His biggest fear was what it might do to them when he told them. He was afraid the news would kill his ailing grandmother. It could possibly cause his father to have a heart attack, and his mother to go into a deep depression. He could not believe that he could fall for a scam like he did. It seemed so real and no risk at all. Think it can't happen to you, think again.

Story 8:

We received word a money manager for a prestigious family had lost over 80% of the family's fortune. He was so despondent over this loss, he committed suicide. This in turn caused his immediate family to lose everything they owned, and they had to move back with other family members to survive. What little they have left barely sustains them after all the costs incurred with his death, burial and estate taxes.

Story 9:

There was a young widow whose husband was killed in a car accident. While she had wisely sought the counsel of a financial planner and had made some prudent investments, a dear family friend told her about this incredible investment program he had joined; and how much money he was making for the past six months. Since she trusted him and had seen his bank deposits of the money he had received from this program, she jumped in with $50,000 of her own. Within days of her funds being deposited into this program the program collapsed. The admin had closed the program and had run with the money. Money she had planned on using for her children's college education fund. Sadly she was not alone. A few others mentioned on the investment forum they had lost far more than the $50,000, and some admitted depositing $100,000 - $250,000 just days before this collapsed; losing it all.

By now I hope you have gotten the picture that it is far more than money that is lost in these scams. These stories represent hundreds of the same stories that happen every day because of people becoming victims of scams. The human and emotional toll is far greater than the financial toll these scams cause.

Every day countless stories are told about people losing their house because they lost it all in a scam, or they are losing their house and car, and as seen some can't handle it and take their own life. The truly sad part is the persons running these scams have no conscious of the pain, suffering and misery they cause. They are almost always a sociopath, as are the people who willingly promote these scams. This has been proven by those who claim they will refund all those who were in their program who were not in profit, and after getting everyone's hopes up it will happen, just walk away with absolutely no guilt. Talk about rubbing salt in the wound.

Next, what the Scammer is asking you to believe.

What the Scammer Is Asking You To Believe

In the past chapters, I have explained and illustrated most of the most common scams being run today on the Internet, how you can protect yourself by heeding our red flag warnings and how to do basic due diligence, explained who the players are, how they do it, the human toll that these scams cause, and now it is time to shine the light on what a scammer is asking you to believe for you to join one of these scams. You see they prey on the fact you will not do any due diligence, or you will seek outside advise. They want you caught up in the moment from all the euphoria that is generated on all the financial forums how this is your chance at the brass ring, and you will become rich with their program. That is the thumbnail version, but here is what they are really asking you to believe and do:

Story 1: A self-touted financial investor has developed a program that will enable you to invest very little money but receive incredible returns. Not only is he able to do this for himself, he is now willing to do it for you too. You are just lucky you have discovered his program and to be one of many who are making a fortune using his program.

Story 2: A multimillionaire on the Internet is going to allow you, an anonymous web-surfer, to share in his program and become rich too. And in both scenarios, they cannot share with you how they do it, or provide you any audited financial statements proving they can.

Story 3: An individual claims he has discovered a way in which he can consistently earn 20%-40% interest on a monthly basis. Rather than keep all this wealth to himself, he is allowing anyone who finds his website to do the same. Never mind that you are a total unknown entity to him, as long as you are living and breathing you qualify for this investment. No silly qualified investor questionnaires needed. No pre-screening of any kind. As long as you have $25 to invest, you qualify. Oh and your principal is GUARANTEED.

Not only is this person from either story above going to do all of this investing for you, he is also going to monitor his own forum, handle all the customer service issues and all the bookkeeping required, and maintain the membership database. In short, he is Superman, the Grand Multi-Tasker of all time, and The Shadow all rolled into one. I think I may have just dated myself, but I have only heard about 'The Shadow.' That's my story and I am sticking to it.

Think about this. When you invest online:

- You are really sending your money to a total stranger whom you have no clue who they really are;
- You are sending money through a payment processor that charges excessive fees to handle your money.
- You have absolutely no control over your money once it has been sent.
- They have no address or phone number for their company for you to contact them;
- They use free E-mail accounts for communication, and many times they are running more than one scam at-a-time, and you don't even know it.
- They also do not reveal their real names, and when they do provide a bio it is fake.
- They do not show any proof they are licensed and registered any- where.
- They either claim they are, or they claim because they are offshore and on the Internet they are not required to be licensed and registered.
- You never receive any audited financial statements nor confirmation of your investment trading.
- You do not receive a monthly or quarterly statement showing the ac- tivity in your account and all the trades made.
- They make outrageous earning or investment return claims with no documentation to support it.

Remember when I said early on in the book these scammers play on despera- tion? Well here is another way they do it:

You receive a call or an E-mail from a friend, or family member, who tells you about this great investment opportunity they are participating in, they are getting paid just like clock-work and receiving 15% monthly on their investment. They don't want you to miss the boat and you should join. They joined because someone else has been in the program for over a year, and they have never had a payment missed. Then they tell you that you cannot lose and this is a no-brainer.

By the way, when you do join you can get others to sign-up under you, and the program will pay you a referral fee just for getting others to join. A total win-win situation for everyone or so it seems. They either show you their results, or they tell you how much they have made on their investment since joining. You don't want to be on the sidelines of such a great deal, and besides you need extra income to cover the losses from your 401(k) or IRA investments.

Then they tell you the famous "your principal is guaranteed" line, and of course it is prominently displayed on the programs website. You really need this extra income since your other investments are not doing that well, and you are not sure how things will turn out at work since the company is also experiencing hard times. So fear of not getting in and missing out especially if a family member is invested (we can't have a family member getting ahead of us financially); takes over common sense and you can't join fast enough and sending as much money as you can,

If you have not learned anything else up until now, I hope you learn this. Before you jump into any program, do the math, ask a lot of questions, do not invest in anything you do not understand or know how it works, seek outside expert advice, and "I've Got Paid" is not Due Diligence.

Next, how can I stop all that spam in my Inbox.

How Can I Stop All The Spam In My Inbox?

You can stop a lot of the spam you receive in your E-mail Inbox just by learning how to forward an E-mail the proper way. Another way is to not answer any E-mail from anyone you don't know. Just delete it. But the biggest culprit of your receiving E-mail spam is you. And you do it unknowingly.

If you are like most people, you get an E-mail from a friend and it is something you want to share with your other friends and family too. So you just hit the forward key, and put in all the E-mail addresses you want to send this information. They in turn receive it, and they also want to share it with their other friends and family so they too hit the forward button and off it goes.

Now we have all received E-mails where you have to scroll down to get to the "whatever" it is they wanted you to see and read because there are at least 3" of all those forwards before it got to you. Many times there are over 150 E-mail addresses before you get to the subject matter you were to read or see. All it takes is just one person's E-mail to have a spyware attachment or a virus, and everyone from that point forward their computer is infected and they don't even know it. While many now have a virus protector on their system, many do not have software to prevent spyware and malware from being attached to your E-mails.

Instead what you need to do is copy the information in the E-mail that you want to forward, and then hit forward and enter the addresses of those you want to see the article. Then you just paste the article in the body of the E-mail. Anyone receiving the E-mail from you does not have to scroll down layers of E-mail addresses to read or see your article, but more importantly they do not have to worry about being infected with spyware or malware.

Any time you see an email that says "forward this on to '10' (or however many) of your friends", "sign this petition", or "you'll get bad luck" or "you'll get good luck" or "you'll see something funny on your screen after you send it" or whatever --- it almost always has an email tracker program attached that tracks the cookies and emails of the people you forward it to. The host sender is getting a copy each time it gets forwarded and then is able to get lists of 'active' email addresses to use in SPAM emails or sell to other spammers. Even when you get emails that demand you send the email **on if you're not ashamed of God/Jesus** --- that is email tracking, and they are playing on our conscience. These people don't care how they get your email addresses - just as long as they get them. Also, emails that talk about a missing child or a child with an incurable disease "how would you feel if that was your child" --- email tracking. Ignore them and don't participate!

Email petitions are NOT acceptable to Congress, Parliament or any other organization - i.e. social security, etc. To be acceptable, petitions must have a "*signed signature*" and full address of the person signing the petition, so this is a waste of time and you are just helping the email trackers.

Just think, no longer does a scammer have to wonder if an E-mail is valid by waiting on a return reply. He now has a database of real live E-mails that all of you have conveniently provided him all because everyone didn't stop and think of the consequences of forwarding the must see or read article.

Remember most outside spam is sent to you bcc so they use a blast effect from an E-mail list they have purchased. Until you respond, they don't know if the E-mail address they bought is a real address or not. If they don't get a reply, they just take your E-mail off the list and stop sending to you. But when you respond, you give them a live E-mail address, and they will use your E-mail address and get around your spam filter.

Ever get an E-mail from the first name of a person you know, so you think it is them; but when you open it you have no clue who it is? Well, they got that name from the list of all those E-mail addresses from when the article was forwarded umpteen times.

By just doing these things, will cut down the spam in your E-mail Inbox by at least 75%. This is another way you can help prevent E-mail fraud from happening to you. Now it is time to sum this all up.

Summing It All Up

I have covered a lot of subjects in this book, and it is my sincere desire that the information contained herein not only has been useful to you, but will also prevent you from ever becoming a victim of any of the Internet investment scams I have talked about. It is amazing to me how people will send thousands, if not hundreds of thousands, of dollars to a total unknown entity or person on the Internet. You only think you know them and who they are.

The key to stopping the majority of these scams it through education. The sole purpose of this book was to educate you about these scams, all the players involved, how they do it, and what they look like so you will immediately recognize one of these scams when you see it. I hope you will refer to this book time and time again to protect yourself from falling for one of these scams, and becoming a victim.

If you follow our Red Flag Warnings, and do basic Due Diligence, you should avoid becoming a victim of these scams. There will still be those times when something is just too tempting for you to refuse, and you will throw all caution to the wind and invest. This is your moment of "gotcha," and they win. Just remember, do not invest more than you can afford to lose. Do not invest money that if you lose it all will cause you any serious financial harm. If you lose it you won't lose your house, your car, not be able to pay your utilities, buy food or gas, make your credit card payments, life/house/car insurance, etc, etc.. Only invest disposable income, but in a small amount. This is just good advice for any investment not just against Internet investment scams.

There are five steps people go through after they have been scammed: 1) Denial, 2) Anger, 3) Bargaining, 4) Depression, and 5) Acceptance. The time it takes to move through all five steps depends on each individual. I know some who never get out of the denial step. Some make it to step 3 Bargaining, but then fall right back to denial. The bottom line is the quicker people can get to step 5, Acceptance, the healthier they will be and recover.

If the FBI Director almost became a victim of a Bank Phishing E-mail Fraud, you can too. If agents and retired agents from federal law enforcement agencies can be victims of a scam, so can you. It makes no difference how much or how little education you have. You can become a victim of a scam. Also remember that the conmen who run these scams are getting better and better at their craft, and making it harder and harder for you to not become a victim. Former Colorado securities commissioner Philip Feigin, now a partner at Denver law firm Rothgerber Johnson & Lyons said: *"People who put together these schemes are very, very good at what they do. Until you listen to some of these pitches, you have no idea how good they are. Anybody who thinks they're too smart to be conned is a likely target."*

Also remember there are no, zip, none, zero, zilch, nada HYIP (High Yield Investment Programs) programs that are offered on the Internet that are legal and not a scam. NOT ONE, in spite of what they claim. There are, however, legitimate HYI (High Yield Investments), but you must qualify to participate. No trader, no matter what anyone claims, can successfully make 2%-3% daily compounded or otherwise for any extended period of time. There are no sports arbitrage bets that are 100% winners every time. Even computer generated systems cannot always have a winning trade or bet 100% of the time.

I know times are tough, and many of you are facing economic uncertainty, but investing in these hyped Internet investment programs is not the way out of your dilemma. You will only end up losing what little money you have left or worse your house and car making matters worse. Even if you are one of the fortunate few who do make money from these scams, you run the risk of having the government taking it all back from claw backs as it is stolen money.

The one thing I have not talked about until now but you need to do is this. If you are a victim of a scam, you must report it. It makes no difference how little or how much you invested they stole. You must show that you were a victim and not an accomplice to the crime. File a complaint with your state Attorney General and also with the IC3 (Internet Crime Complaint Center). Also encourage others who were also victims of the scam to also report it. If you do not live in the U.S., then report it to your country's regulatory agency in charge of investments/securities. The more people reporting it the better the chances are of an investigation being done. I cannot emphasize this enough. If someone robbed you of your money, or stole something out of your car, would you not report it to the police? Of course you would. You would want the thief caught and punished. But with Internet investment scams we let our pride, ego, embarrassment, fear of ridicule by family members or worse, shame, self-condemnation stop us from reporting the crime against us. To paraphrase a dear friend of mine, Annie McGuire, Founder of Fraud Aid, Inc (www.fraudaid.org) : "Silence is a scammer's best friend. Word of mouth is a scammer's worst enemy. Pass the Word!"

It is the only way this epidemic is going to be stopped, and it is an economic epidemic that is destroying economies around the world. The country of Albania had almost 50% of its nation's GDP lost to the collapse of a $1.2 Billion Ponzi scheme. Rioting occurred and 2.000 people were killed, and it toppled the government. The people of Benin are calling for the prosecution of the country's president because of a giant Ponzi scheme that just collapsed there. Riots were held in Colombia because of money lost to another giant Ponzi scheme that collapsed.

Before you think it can't happen to you, think again. You or somebody you know have a 1 in 10 chance of being scammed before the end of 2011. It makes no difference how little or how much education you have, you can be scammed. A conman said he would rather have a room full of Mensa people to make his pitch to than anyone else. He said their ego would not let them admit he didn't know what he was talking about, and they would be an easy mark for his scam. They know how to gain your 'trust.' They make you believe they are your best friend, and only want to help you get ahead financially in life. The people who join these programs will become like family to you. You will exchange E-mails, chat with them on the private forum established for the members of the investment program. They will become your best buddy right up to the time they run with your money and disappear. This is how they do it. They are not called Conmen for nothing. I call them criminals.

Before I end this book, I do want to offer you an investment opportunity for you to consider:

During falling markets or large market corrections banks have massive amounts of funds that sit off ledger and this causes problems for the banks. They need to use a transaction to reduce their exposure but have limits to the size of off ledger funds due to banking regulations. With the recent market crashes I know of a least 2 banks that are happy to offer this transaction to private investors in order to allow them to balance their books.

This is subject to the normal NDAs and proof of funds, the banks have asked to remain confidential to avoid unnecessary attention, however, they are a world top 50 bank underwritten by a Lloyds of London leveraged trading program linked to the LIBOR overnight lending rate.

I have access to one of these trading programs for a minimum $100k. We are looking to raise this through $100 lots with 1000 investors who will need to provide proof of funds and upload a copy of their passport and once approved we will take the first available opportunity to conduct the trade. The profit split will be on a 60/40 basis using a 100-1 leverage thus yielding a $6000 return Once the trading program has completed you will have the oppootunity to roll all or part of the profit into another LTAC and repeat this process for a maximum of another time thus giving the potential to yield a maximum of $360K. 100 X 100 = 10000 @ 60% = 6000. 6000 X 100 = 600000 @60% = 360000.

You have the choice to take your profit at the first program or invest all or part, however, only two investment opportunities per passport application.

You have to understand how intricate all of this is, and it takes time to put all this together. Besides, we have to remain below the radar of any government agencies, and trolls who don't want these type of programs made available to the masses. This is usually reserved for the rich only. It is only because of my extensive contacts within the financial communities that I was even able to put this together. Since we are dealing with the banks, the banking solution is in place. They are forming a private bank just for this program, thus it will be offshore and not subject to any taxes. Because they will open this offshore bank, it will not fall under any legal jurisdictions or securities regulators of any kind.

What is even more exciting is that the offshore bank will be splitting all the profits with those who open accounts with them, and keep part of their money in this account. They will split the profits daily from whatever they make in their investments. The best part is it will only require a minimum balance of $1,500 to get in on this aspect of the deal. Of course they will offer another program just like this once this has paid out. They expect their trading to generate at least 1% daily, thus each account participating will receive 1/2% daily. Some days they may not make 1%, but other days they should make a lot more, possibly as high as 2%. This is a win-win for everyone. At last a chance for the little guy to get wealthy.

Those interested let me know via E-mail, and I'll tell you how this will be done.

How many of you want to contact me to join this program? After all it is a great opportunity, and one you cannot afford not to participate. Think of all the good you will be able to do with the returns you will receive from your participation.

By now you should have been able to spot all the red flag warnings this was not real. At least I hope so. I posted this information on one of the financial forum threads about another investment scam. I told people if they were interested in knowing more about the program to send me a private message. I thought only a handful of people would fall for this, as there are many red flag warnings flying all over the place. It didn't even last a day before I had to announce on the financial forum it was not real. I had more than 500 private messages about people wanting to know more about this program. Now what made this even more remarkable is it was posted in a thread about a program that had just folded proving it was a scam. I hate to think what would have happened if I had let it run for a week. Remember how people are desperate? This is just one more example proving it.

I started this book by asking you a question: Do you believe you can be scammed? I believe your answer then was NO. I hope this book has shown you it can happen to you. Let me end this book by asking you another question: After reading this book do you believe you will **NOT** be scammed?

CONGRATULATIONS! if you answered YES. You won't lose your life savings, your house, your car, or worse to these scammers. I also win because you won't be calling me telling me your horror story of being a victim of a scam.

ABOUT THE AUTHOR

 Lynn Edgington is a graduate of Ball State University with a double major in Business Administration and Political Science, and a minor in Radio-Television.

He has more than twenty years experience in the financial services industry (banking, insurance, mortgage), and more than twenty years experience as a business management consultant and research analyst. These combined work experiences, plus spending four years researching Internet investment scams led to the formation of Eagle Research Associates, Inc.

He is the founder/president of Eagle Research Associates, Inc., a 501(c)3 California Public Benefit Charitable Nonprofit Corporation. Eagle Research Associates was formed with a dual mission:

1. To educate the public about Internet Investment Fraud/Ponzi/Scams. This mission is accomplished by conducting free community seminars, radio-television interviews, newspaper articles, posting on financial forums and blogs, full-day workshops, and information provided on Eagle's website.

2. To provide the research information gathered by Eagle Research Associates on Internet Investment Fraud/Ponzi's/Scams to assigned agents from several federal law enforcement agencies, and law enforcement agencies worldwide. This mission has resulted with Eagle assisting in the shut-down of twenty-two Internet investment scams to date.